CW01032971

Faiths in Higher Education Chaplaincy

Church of England Board of Education
Church House
Great Smith Street
London
SW1P 3AZ

ISBN 978-0-9558096-0-6

Published 2008 by the Church of England Board of Education

Copyright © The Archbishops' Council 2008
Afterword © Rick Trainor 2008
Appendix 5: Building Good Relations with People of Different Faiths and Beliefs ©
The Inter Faith Network for the UK 1993, 2005
Front Cover image: ©iStockphoto.com/Chris Schmidt

All rights reserved. No part of this publication may be reproduced or stored or
transmitted by any means or in any for, electronic or mechanical, including
photocopying, recording, or any information storage or retrieval system without
written permission which should be sought from the Copyright and Contracts
Administrator, The Archbishops' Council, Church of England, Church House,
Great Smith Street, London SW1P 3AZ.
E-mail: copyright@c-of-e.org.uk

Jeremy M S Clines asserts his right under the Copyright, Design and Patents Act,
1988 to be identified as Author of this Work.

This report was funded by the Faith Communities Capacity Building Fund of the
Department of Communities and Local Government. It was commissioned by the
Church of England Board of Education from Jeremy M S Clines, on secondment
from the chaplaincy at York St John University, as a contribution to discussion
about the development of chaplaincy in higher education in England and Wales.

Cover design by Neil Hunter
Typesetting by Iain Beswick

Printed by Lightning Source

Faiths in Higher Education Chaplaincy

Jeremy M S Clines

A report of a project funded by the
Faith Communities Capacity Building Fund
commissioned by the
Church of England Board of Education

Further Copies of this Report

For information about obtaining further copies of this report please write to:

Faiths in Higher Education Chaplaincy
Education Division
Church House
Great Smith Street
London
SW1P 3AZ

Telephone: 0207 898 1505

The Church of England Board of Education offers this report into the discussion about the development of chaplaincy in higher education and expresses its commitment to engage with interested parties—including chaplains, faith communities, higher education institutions and sector agencies—to improve provision.

Contact:

The National Adviser for Higher Education and Chaplaincy
Education Division
Church House
Great Smith Street
London
SW1P 3AZ

Contents

Contents

Preface

During 2006 and 2007 the Church of England hosted what has come to be known as the *Faiths in Higher Education Chaplaincy* project, commissioned by the Board of Education and based in the Education Division, but relating as far as possible to all chaplaincies in England and Wales, and to all nine major faith communities. This project has set out to examine the engagement of the faiths in higher education chaplaincy and to reflect on the development of chaplaincies in order to further the involvement of the faiths in higher education. What follows in these pages is a record of what took place and a description of what was discovered together with key questions for further consideration by chaplains, higher education institutions and the faith communities themselves.

What has been discovered through a significant and sustained process of consultation will, I hope, prove beneficial for all of us whose task is to reflect together on the shape of chaplaincy in our higher education institutions in the future. I would like to put on record right at the start my thanks to all who have supported this work so generously from across the faith communities and the higher education sector, whether through giving time to answer the telephone survey, attend dialogues, script narratives or through the countless conversations and words of support and encouragement which have been offered along the way.

It is important to state clearly that although the project was hosted by the Church of England, it did not have the Church of England's work in higher education chaplaincy as its primary focus. A successful funding bid to the Faith Communities Capacity Building Fund (FCCBF) set out four main purposes:

- o to identify the participation of different faith communities in university chaplaincies;
- o to identify different chaplaincy models which have developed or are developing;
- o to make recommendations for best practice to enable the most effective inter faith participation, collaboration and activity;
- o and to disseminate findings to faith communities, universities and interested parties throughout England and Wales.

What follows in this volume is therefore addressed to all interested parties, including the Church of England; and the Church of England, along with others, will want to put energy into thinking through what has been discovered and considering its response.

For the avoidance of any doubt, it is important to state here something of the motivation for initiating this particular project, both in terms of the Church's position as regards inter faith work, and as regards higher education chaplaincy.

In partnership with other Christian churches, the Church of England seeks to build up good relations with people of other faith traditions, and to cooperate with them where possible in service to society. Back in 1981, the General Synod endorsed the *Four Principles of Inter-faith Dialogue* agreed ecumenically by the British Council of Churches, recognising the significant changes which have led to religious plurality in our society:

o   Dialogue begins when people meet each other
o   Dialogue depends upon mutual understanding and mutual trust
o   Dialogue makes it possible to share in service to the community
o   Dialogue becomes the medium of authentic witness

The Anglican commitment to working ecumenically in inter faith relations remains unequivocal.

As far as chaplaincy in higher education is concerned, in 2005 the General Synod expressed its wholehearted support of chaplains in this area of its ministry. It recognised the key role of chaplains in higher education in their work, based on the principle that where possible the Church of England should strive to ensure full time chaplaincy provision in higher education institutions.

The Church of England's bid to the FCCBF arose out of its experience of its chaplains working in almost every higher education institution, and of emerging models of chaplaincy. Its conviction is that wider representation of the faith communities in chaplaincies is essential to ensure that the faith needs of students, staff and institutions are met, that the possibilities of inter faith working are increased, and that each of our faith communities can speak with integrity in a context of open dialogue. All these factors help embed chaplaincies in the life of the institutions which they serve.

On the one hand, a particular question for us as the established Church in England is what it means to be there "for all faiths and none", especially when many in university communities are from a variety of world faith communities, and faith is arguably on the agenda in higher education institutions more than it has been for a long time. This is especially the case at a time when in general there has been a move, at least in some places, from an awareness, to a tolerance, to a celebration of difference. Yet, at the same time, world events have caused some to look at religious diversity rather more warily. John Austin, the former Bishop of Aston, described the term *Presence and Engagement* as 'a beautifully succinct way of expressing our dilemma and suggesting an answer' in his foreword to the Church report of the same name, sub-titled *The Churches' task in a multi Faith society* — which focussed on work in parishes. The Church of England, other denominational and faith colleagues, have seen our role supporting higher education institutions in recognising and adapting to their ever more diverse populations as increasingly important. I dare suggest that here, too, the potential benefits of our collective presence and engagement are very great indeed.

At the same time, as members of a particular faith community themselves, Christians believe that they have their part to play in the lives of universities and colleges, which have the freedom to pursue truth at their heart, bringing a particular Christian perspective to the conversations that arise. But we explicitly want to do that alongside others, and we want others to have the opportunity to express their own faith or beliefs as well. We value enormously the role that Christian chaplains have been able to play in the past and we are committed to serving institutions by ensuring that faith needs of all students and staff are met as fully as possible. We recognise, as members of the Church in the "public square", that we have a responsibility to ensure that people with different needs have access to those who can support them, but also that sometimes our own chaplains are not best placed to enable that to happen.

We also recognise that in the ever more diverse world of higher education two things are becoming increasingly important for members of the faith communities to do together. First, we should work together, which will enable us to put our own points of view not just because we have always done so or because we have a particular platform, but because we do so in a context where each is encouraged to be authentically themselves and to speak with integrity. This is not about "watering down" convictions or glossing over difference. It is certainly not about suggesting that someone without an allegiance to a particular faith community could in some way serve everyone's needs by being there as a lone 'multi-faith chaplain' (which is why for some the term 'multi-faith chaplaincy' is problematic). The contention is that for a chaplain to work alongside chaplains of other faiths will actually liberate them to be themselves, each being freed to express their own faith in the context of open dialogue. This will serve Christian chaplains well, as it will serve others.

Second, those working together as members of extended teams in chaplaincies in higher education, drawn as they are from various faith communities, have a wonderful and important opportunity to model good inter faith relationships. At a time when 43% of our 18–30 year olds are entering higher education, it must surely be the case that the relationships they forge and the strategies they learn as they encounter diversity and difference are going to help form the attitudes they will take with them into the rest of their lives. If, as we in the Church of England Board of Education would maintain, higher education has a higher purpose, which is the development of the whole person, then surely we ignore this opportunity at our peril, and would be negligent if we did not seek to take full advantage of it.

On behalf of the Board of Education a few words of thanks: to the FCCBF for its funding of the project; to Jeremy Clines, Chaplain at York St John University for all his work as the project officer even after his secondment was formally over; to Professor Dianne Willcocks, Vice-Chancellor of York St John University for agreeing to his secondment; and to all those who contributed to the project in many different ways. I would like to make special mention of those drawn from the Baha'i, Buddhist, Christian, Hindu, Jain, Jewish, Muslim and Sikh faith communities who have served as a reference group during the project: Fatma Amer, Aviva Dautch, Adam Dawson, Gerry Devlin, Jay Lakhani, Barney Leith, Sam McBratney, Melinda Michelson-Carr, Mudita, Susan O'Brien, Mohammed Rafi, Natubhai Shah, Kanwaljit Kaur-Singh, Chris Ward and Judith Williams. Most were able to attend an important day conference organised by Jeremy Clines and Hugh Shilson-Thomas (the Church of England's National Adviser for Higher Education and Chaplaincy) to review the project process and outcomes to date and set a steer for the remainder of the work. Several also served as critical readers of parts of the draft text, together with Harriet Crabtree (Inter Faith Network), Moussa Haddad (Equality Challenge Unit), Alice Hynes (GuildHE) and Catherine Marston (UniversitiesUK). Their collective input to the project has been invaluable.

The Right Revd Dr Kenneth Stevenson
Chairman, Church of England Board of Education

December 2007

Acknowledgements

It has been a privilege to work on a project that was intended as a collaborative one, since I believe that it is in shared experience that inter religious co-operation is most successful. My first thanks go to Hugh Shilson-Thomas who not only conceived the project and won the bid, but has served as mid-wife to my endeavours as author and project officer. Next my thanks go to the many people who have participated; there are over 200! This turned the aspiration that the project would be an opportunity for deepened mutual understanding into reality and ensured that all of us have both taught and learnt through our dialogue.

I am grateful too to the many other staff of the Education Division who have contributed some of their time to the project: Jan Ainsworth, Pat Barton, Daryl Booth, Liz Carter, Steven Cooper, John Hall, Jo Hibbert, Steve Jenkins, Alan Murray, Enrique Ramos and Ben Wilson. Thanks also to Ailsa Parkin at Sheffield Phoenix Press for her advice and liaison, to Neil Hunter for the cover design and Iain Beswick for the typesetting.

My gratitude for what has helped make this work possible stretches back to the 1970s when my mum and dad gave me the chance as a seven- and eight- year old to spend time at the Society of Friends Quaker Central Meeting House in Sheffield where reading contemporary fables shaped my understanding about mutuality and co-operation.

The time I spent in 1997 at the Irish School of Ecumenics studying issues in inter faith relations was a vital chance to further my thinking: I am indebted, therefore, to the tutors and students I learnt with, and also to the Spalding Trust, the Diocese of York and Cranmer Hall who made the four months there possible.

There are three posthumous acknowledgements I want to give for the inspiration that has gone into this report: they are to John Austin, Roger Hooker and Michael Vasey. They each, through their tailor-made approach to my ministerial formation, regarding inter faith issues, have enabled me to think for myself while depending on their strength of wisdom.

More recently, the support of my Vice- Chancellor, Dianne Willcocks, has helped me to the place where I was suitably equipped to undertake this project activity — first through her support of me in establishing an inter faith team in 2003 at York St John and then giving me the opportunity to take on the seconded work at the Education Division.

It is the York St John Faith Advisors, though, who have been my most significant educators, since over four years I have learnt so much about all the faiths they represent, including my own. They have gently helped me to uncover a whole host of my own preconceptions too. They are; Zubair Ahmed, Hooshmand and May Badee, Barbara and Geoffrey Cantor, Darminder Singh Chadha and Gurdeep Kaur Chadha, Mohamed el Gomati, Pauline Kollontai, Huma Rahman, David and Mary Smith, Kelsang Chöchin, Mahendra and Usha Verma and Nicola Williams.

I'm glad that my colleagues Sharon Lusty and Priscilla Preston along with Chris Cullwick were so encouraging to me despite being the ones left behind to cover my secondment, and I'm grateful that they have continued to cheer me on when I've been hiding away preparing the report for publication.

A thousand thanks to my wife Louise and the Clines/McKay, Grace-Clement, Granthier, Norwood, Reynolds and Shilson-Thomas house-olds.

Jeremy Clines
10 December 2007

1. Introduction

This introductory section outlines the work of the project and the process by which this report has been produced.

A full list of project participants, chaplaincies contacted and faith community representatives who have played a key role in steering the work is provided in the appendices.

A. The Church of England Education Division bid to the FCCBF

In 2006 the Church of England Education Division (on behalf of the Church of England Board of Education) made a successful bid to the Faith Communities Capacity Building Fund (FCCBF) that funds projects in England and Wales. The bid was for a project looking at the development of chaplaincies to further the involvement of the world faiths in higher education (HE) in England and Wales. This was in response to the observations that many chaplaincies in Higher Education institutions (HEIs) now list a range of chaplains or advisors drawn from various faith communities as part of their extended teams, and that a range of models and practice is developing. The Church of England believed that all those involved in the support and provision of chaplaincy would benefit from a sustained reflection on emerging ways of working.

B. The Project proposal

The proposal stated that the project would

- o identify the participation of different faith communities in HEI chaplaincies
- o identify different chaplaincy models which have developed or are developing
- o make recommendations for best practice to enable most effective inter faith participation, collaboration and activity
- o disseminate findings to faith communities, HEIs and interested parties throughout England and Wales.

C. Project Officer

The funding enabled the secondment of Jeremy Clines as HE Chaplaincy Development Officer in the Education Division, who was appointed to work full-time on the project for seven months from September 2006 to March 2007 and to write a report for dissemination in fulfilment of the project's aims. In this work he has referred very widely to chaplains, university and college management and faith community representatives as well as others in organisations with interests in the work. These have together provided a collective steer, with a group of nominated faith community representatives offering specific guidance during the project process (see Appendix 2). On a day-to-day basis, Jeremy liaised closely with Hugh Shilson-Thomas, the Church of England's National Adviser for Higher Education and Chaplaincy, who served as his line manager in the Education Division for the period of his secondment, and with whom he shaped the project. In the event Jeremy continued to work on the project beyond his formal secondment in order to bring the report to publication by the end of 2007.

As Chaplain of York St John University for eight years prior to commencing the secondment, Jeremy had established a team of Faith Advisors consisting of a man and woman from each of seven world faiths. He therefore came to the project with both chaplaincy experience and credibility within the faith communities.

D. The consultation process

Initial consultation began with representatives from across the faith communities currently engaged in chaplaincy work in the higher education context. Informal discussions about the project were held at this early stage with chaplains, faith advisors, students, student workers and others with an interest in the development of chaplaincy.

D1 Visits

Initial visits were made to eight Higher Education institutions to talk with chaplaincy members and student faith society leaders.

D2 Wider consultation

A wider consultation was begun with the faith communities. The Inter Faith Network for the UK (IFN) provided support and advice on establishing appropriate contacts. Project briefings were sent to representatives of the nine main faith communities in the UK. These nine faiths are, Baha'i, Buddhism, Christianity, Hinduism, Jainism, Judaism, Sikhism and Zoroastrianism. These faith representatives were asked to identify key partners in the project to ensure as full collaboration and partnership as possible. They were also invited to nominate appropriate people to attend a key meeting in February 2007 to review the work to date and give feedback on the project activity, as well as to guide the project to its completion by making recommendations for further work and offering guidance on what to include in the final report.

D3 Critical Readers

Those who subsequently attended that meeting were added to a list of critical readers asked to review the draft Project Results which were circulated to faith representatives and other interested parties prior to the final report being completed and prepared for publication. The Project Results include most of the principal implications of the report; however some further implications are raised in 'Conclusions and Next Steps' and consequently some further consultation on this chapter took place just prior to publication.

D4 Further contacts

Contacts were established with representatives of national student faith organisations and with the National Union of Students. Their input to the seven regional practice workshops was especially encouraged.

D5 Vice- Chancellors and Principals

All Vice- Chancellors and Principals in England and Wales were sent a briefing about the project and responses were invited. For the sake of a wider perspective, Heads of HEIs in Scotland were sent a similar briefing and invited to respond. Similar briefings were sent to at least one chaplain in every known chaplaincy. Those who received these briefings were asked to share the information with ecumenical and other faith colleagues.

D6 Other religious and belief perspectives

This report focuses on the involvement of the nine faith communities in HE chaplaincy. There are other religious and belief perspectives that are held, by students and staff, within the HEI sector. How those perspectives are engaged with is something for HEIs, Equality and Diversity departments, chaplaincies and students and staff themselves to consider. This report does occasionally touch on issues that relate to religious and belief perspectives beyond those of the Baha'i, Buddhist, Christian, Hindu, Jain, Jewish, Muslim, Sikh and Zoroastrian religions. However, it is the involvement of the world religions in chaplaincies that is the primary focus of this report and questions about the involvement in chaplaincy work by those with other religious and belief perspectives (for example, members of New Religious Movements) is beyond the remit of this particular study.

E. Survey of chaplaincies in England and Wales

Contact was attempted with all HEI chaplaincies by telephone survey to determine the current participation of different faith communities in university chaplaincies in England and Wales. Contact was made with chaplaincies that serve 111 of the 128 HEIs in existence in England and Wales at the time of the survey. No contact was achieved with ten further chaplaincies. The remaining seven HEIs had no chaplaincy provision at the time of the survey.

E1 Number of chaplaincy responses

From the chaplaincies contacted, survey results have been collected from 104 HEI chaplaincies that, at the time of the survey, were serving at 105 HEIs. Two of these survey returns are intentionally omitted in the collated survey results in this report (see below). The results of the telephone survey were written up and sent to the interviewees for checking and amendment where necessary.

Altogether 92% of operational HEI chaplaincies were contacted, 86% were surveyed and 84% of all chaplaincies are included in the published results. The 102 chaplaincies included in the final results operated at 103 HEIs in England and Wales.

These results provide a unique overview of faith activity in Higher Education through HE chaplaincies.

E2 The universities of Cambridge, Durham, London, Oxford and Wales

Contact was made with HEI chaplaincies at Cambridge, Durham, London and Oxford and visits made to three of these four. Chaplaincy practitioners from all these institutions participated in the project and students from some of these institutions were involved. Data was collected for Oxford and Cambridge as part of the survey, but these findings have been omitted here since in nearly every instance the constituent colleges' chaplaincies work independently of one another and consequently many of the survey questions were irrelevant. Because of the high level of chaplaincy provision in those colleges combined with the requirement by Statute in the great majority of colleges for that provision to be Christian and Anglican, it was decided that to include data for all colleges in Oxford and Cambridge would have led to a misleading picture of overall provision.

Durham is included in the survey data since its religious and belief provision, chaplaincy staffing levels and physical prayer spaces are more commensurate with other HEIs than with Oxford and Cambridge. The institutions that make up the universities of London and Wales were treated as separate institutions in line with the practice of the funding councils in England and Wales, and are included separately in the survey results.

F. Site visits and Practice Narratives

The Development Officer completed visits to 24 HEI chaplaincies. During the visit to each chaplaincy and its HEI, there was usually an opportunity to meet with other members of staff, faith representatives and students of different faiths. Arising from these visits, practice narratives were composed between the Development Officer and the chaplaincy practitioner visited. These practice narratives are included in the project results.

G. Practice Dialogues

Seven regional practice workshops took place between 29 January and 9 February 2007, where practitioners working in, or associated with, HE chaplaincy met together to discuss a range of themes pre-planned by the Development Officer. Information inviting expressions of interest was circulated very widely to chaplains, universities and colleges and student faith societies in order to ensure that representation was as wide as possible. To allow for further development of these dialogues between practitioners, a web-based discussion of the topics was set up that included the contributions from the day workshops. This ensured that all interested parties contacted had an opportunity to participate in the research by contributing views on chaplaincy models, higher education institution best practice in relation to religion and belief, and inter faith working in relation to the HE context. 76 practitioners participated in the dialogues, including five from Scottish HEIs.

H. The Report

This report contains a combination of research of current provision (quantitative analysis) and research of activities in the 'field' (qualitative critique).

H1 Findings

In the findings the report explores exemplary practice, shares practitioners' expertise, and offers a new map of the terrain of inter religious working in HE chaplaincies.

H2 Recommendations

Recommendations arising from the findings are made. These suggest approaches for improved working for HEIs, routes to enhancing the activities of HEI chaplaincies, and opportunities for effective engagement by the faith communities themselves.

H3 For further consideration

Suggestions are made for further consideration with current exemplary practice serving as the foundation from which new developments and improvements can be made to existing provision.

H4 Conclusions and Next Steps

The 'Findings', 'Recommendations' and suggestions 'For Further Consideration' are relevant to chaplaincies, HEI managers, the faith communities, Students' Unions, student faith societies and others interested in how the world faiths are engaging in higher education through chaplaincies. They are summarised in the conclusion.

I. Faith Communities Capacity Building Fund (FCCBF)

FCCBF funding comes from the Cohesion and Faiths Unit (CFU), which was formerly part of the Home Office. Changes in government structure meant that the CFU, part of the Race, Cohesion and Faiths

Directorate, moved to the Department for Communities and Local Government (DCLG). The DCLG combines responsibility for equality policy, housing, urban regeneration, planning and local government in one department. It has a remit to promote community cohesion, and is made up of the Race, Cohesion and Faiths Directorate, the Women and Equality Unit and the new Commission for Equality and Human Rights. The FCCBF fund itself is administered by the Community Development foundation. See www.cdf.org.uk for further details.

2. Project Results

A. Survey Results

A1 Chaplaincy nomenclature

Chaplaincy title	Responses
Chaplaincy	79
Multi-faith Chaplaincy	9
Ecumenical Chaplaincy	4
Chapel	1
Pastoral Services	1
Chaplaincy and Spiritual Care	1
Anglican Chaplaincy	1
Chaplain	2
Chaplains, Faith and Advisor Team	1
No name	3

Findings
Of the chaplaincies surveyed, 92% (94) include the word 'chaplaincy' in their name. Of those that use the name 'chaplaincy', 82% use the single word as the title. Just fewer than 10% (9) of the survey use the term 'Multi-faith'. 4% use the term 'Ecumenical', describing the formal involvement of several different Christian denominations working together. Some chaplaincies, which had previously used that title, have now changed their name to 'Multi-faith Chaplaincy' to reflect their chaplaincy's diversity.

Recommendations
Although it is of merit that some have opted for more complex titles such as 'Multi-faith Chaplaincy', 'Pastoral Services' and 'Chaplaincy and Spiritual Care' to clarify what their work is about, it is quite likely that the longer the title, the greater possible number of semantic debates that can be generated by a service's name. A chaplaincy shows its diversity by the range of staff employed more than by its title.

The title 'chaplaincy' may well be perceived as explicitly Christian by some, while some in other faith communities use this term as their own. Rather than eliminating this standard form of nomenclature, as some have decided to do, there is a case for a fuller debate about what the title means and evidence of how it is being used in the contexts where it is used. At this time 'multi-faith' cannot be regarded as the preferred title for a chaplaincy.

For further consideration
There are contrasting pressures to change a chaplaincy's nomenclature. First, that a new title will improve the perception of the service. Second, that a new name will lead to an improvement of the service. Third, that the practice in other areas of chaplaincy should lead the way, for example, hospitals, prisons and the armed services. It is worth considering whether a name change is necessary, and if so, what the aim of change may be, especially since the words 'chaplaincy', 'multi-faith' and 'ecumenical' will have different meanings to different people at an HEI.

A2 Number of full-time salaried staff per chaplaincy

Number of f-t staff	Responses
0	26
1	36
2	18
3	17
4	2
5	1
6	0
7	2

Findings
There are 150 full-time staff in chaplaincies in the HEIs surveyed. 75% of HEI chaplaincies have one or more full-time salaried members of staff. There are more chaplaincies with two or more full-time members of staff (40) than there are with only one (36). Whether appointments are full-time is related, in part, to at least some of the following:

- o   the foundation of the institution(s)
- o   the financial commitment of the institution(s)
- o   the financial commitment of faith communities
- o   the size of the institution(s).

Recommendations
See below (A4) for 'Recommendations' arising from tables A2 to A4.

For further consideration
See below (A4) for matters 'For further consideration' arising from tables A2 to A4.

A3 HEI chaplaincies with part-time salaried staff

Number of p-t staff	Responses
0	35
1	21
2	15
3	14
4	5
5	3
6	3
7	4
8	1
15	1

Findings

There are 47 more part-time staff (197) than there are full time staff (150) working in the HEI chaplaincies surveyed. Four of the 102 chaplaincies have no salaried staff at all. There are eight chaplaincies where there are only part-time staff and no voluntary or full-time salaried staff.

59% (45) of the 76 HEI chaplaincies with full-time staff also have part-time staff. 85% (22) of the 26 HEI chaplaincies with no full-time staff have part-time staff. Of the 197 part-time salaried staff in the chaplaincies surveyed, 138 of them work in 45 chaplaincies alongside full-time staff and 57 of them do not have full-time colleagues. In these 45 chaplaincies where part-time staff are working alongside full-time colleagues there is an average of 3 part-time staff per chaplaincy. At the 22 chaplaincies with part-time salaried staff and no full-time staff, the average is 2.7 part-time staff.

Recommendations

See below (A4) for 'Recommendations' arising from tables A2 to A4.

For further consideration

See below (A4) for matters 'For further consideration' arising from tables A2 to A4.

A4 Chaplaincies with voluntary chaplaincy staff

Number of voluntary staff	Responses
0	26
1	14
2	9
3	11
4	9
5	10
6	2
7	6
8	7
9	1
10	2
12	2
13	1
16	1
18	1
19	1

Findings
Volunteers are a normal part of chaplaincy staff teams. There are 371 volunteers (52% of all chaplaincy staff) as compared with 347 part-time and full-time salaried staff. 59 chaplaincies with full-time staff also have volunteers; there are 292 voluntary staff working in these locations. There are a further 17 chaplaincies with full-time salaried staff but no voluntary staff.

Where a chaplaincy has both full-time staff and volunteers, the voluneers are present at an average of 5.0 volunteers per chaplaincy. Eight volunteers work in four chaplaincies without any salaried staff, at an average of two volunteers per chaplaincy. 69 of the volunteers work in 22 chaplaincies where there are salaried part-time staff and no full-time salaried staff, at an average of 3.1 volunteers per chaplaincy. 26 chaplaincies have no voluntary staff.

Recommendations (Tables A2–A4)
In the light of the successes HEI chaplaincies have had in recent years in obtaining further funding (see Table A14) it is timely that chaplaincies without either full-time, part-time or voluntary staff should consider with local faith communities how staffing can be increased. It is worth noting the significant number of voluntary staff already representing faith communities within chaplaincy teams (see Table A5 for further details).

There are more part-time chaplaincy staff than full-time staff. Much of the training of chaplains happens at national or regional level, often at residential meetings. These numbers suggest new challenges to those planning training opportunities for part-time staff who are less able to access learning opportunities that are residential or whole-day. This same issue is magnified for those volunteering. Their hours are likely to be more occasional and they will have fewer chances to attend training.

For further consideration (Tables A2-A4)
A range of information was collected from practitioners during the research project about volunteers within chaplaincy teams (see Section B, Dialogues B2.1-B2.4). Several issues are faced, first by those who are voluntary members of teams, and secondly, by the salaried staff who, typically, lead them. Significant issues include:

- o   training needs
- o   a clarity of role within the team
- o   recruitment of staff
- o   job descriptions
- o   relationships with local faith communities
- o   provision of working spaces.

HEI chaplaincies that as yet have no voluntary team members (26%) will benefit from learning from the 74% of chaplaincies that do have volunteers, prior to determining their own practice. There is a significant opportunity for those without volunteers to consider the experience of others (see the following narratives in Section C: C7, C12, C13, C15 and C16). In addition visits to chaplaincies with volunteers could prove to be very valuable. Appropriately designed training events that could be accessed by team leaders would be timely, as well as training that could be developed for use at a local level with volunteers.

A5 Religion or belief of chaplaincy staff

Religion or belief of staff	staff	*f-t*	*p-t*	*vol*	links	total
Baha'i	7			*7*	2	9
Buddhist	19			*19*	8	27
Christian	543	*143*	*155*	*245*	79	622
Hindu	13		*1*	*12*	11	24
Jewish	40		*9*	*31*	31	71

Religion or belief of staff	staff	f-t	p-t	vol	links	total
Muslim	41	1	5	35	18	59
Sikh	10			10	8	18
Other religious/belief identity	10	1		9	4	14
Role not faith related	34	5	27	2	0	34
Religion not stated	1			1	4	5
Total number of people	718	150	197	371	165	883

Findings

Of 718 staff, 78% of all religious appointments to chaplaincies are Christian. The next largest number is Muslim (6%) and Jewish (6%). The fourth largest category is posts where religion is not role related (5%); this includes positions such as administrators, cleaners and gardeners.

Of the 150 full-time salaried staff, 95% (143) have a Christian role (usually as a chaplain or chaplaincy assistant). Five full-time staff are in posts where the role is not faith related. Of the 197 part-time salaried staff 79% (155) are Christian positions, 8% (15) are posts representing religions other than Christianity and 14% (27) are posts where religion is not role related. Of the 371 voluntary staff 66% (245) are Christian, 33% (124) represent religions other than Christianity, 1% (2) are where religion is not role related, and less than 1% (1) is a post where the person's religion is not stated.

The category 'Other religious/belief identity' refers to any religious or belief view not included in the list of nine faiths (or world religions) presented in the introduction to this report. Although there was an opportunity for respondents to include beliefs that would not come under the category of a religious view, for example, humanism or atheism, no data was provided for people working in such a capacity.

When links between the chaplaincy and a local religious representative are included in the total figures, 70% of staff and links are Christian, 26% of staff and links represent religions other than Christianity and 4% are posts where role is not faith related. The definition of a link comes from the question asked in the survey, 'In addition to the staff are there other contacts, links or external advisors that are advertised as part of your service; if so, how many?' Overall engagement by the faiths other than Christian, including links, sits at 26%: Baha'i, 1%; Buddhist, 3%; Hindu 3%; Jewish, 8%; Muslim, 7%; Sikh, 2%; Other Religion, 2%.

Recommendations

The significant numbers of links, volunteers and part-time staff in HE chaplaincies is impressive. It is also remarkable that the very large majority of staff is Christian, despite the opportunities created for volunteers to join teams. Sometimes the local context may make it unrealistic for a local representative to be found to support a student from a particularly small faith group. In these instances a chaplaincy that is working to serve all HEI members should be able to support that person in their spiritual development and be a signposting service too.

It is important that the reasons for levels of volunteering from diverse faith communities, in individual contexts, should be explored. Chaplaincies and those responsible for equality and diversity issues at HEIs look carefully at how religious perspectives are currently being represented and whether positive adjustments need to be made either in the chaplaincy or elsewhere in the institution.

The research activity for this project has revealed that there are some people – and at least one or two currently or recently working in higher education chaplaincy – who identify themselves as 'interfaith ministers'. This identification is based on a different understanding of the relationship between faith communities.

An authorised minister within a world religion might see themselves as being available to everyone, but is nonetheless rooted explicitly in their own faith tradition, and in the great majority of cases authorised by and accountable to their faith community. An 'interfaith minister', on the other hand, might see himself or herself as trained to work across all religions. This accreditation is not one that is given by a recognised faith community, but rather by those who offer training for the particular role of 'interfaith minister'. However, it should be noted that this approach would not be acceptable to any of the faith communities.

The recommendation arising out of the research for this report is that the guidance offered by the Inter Faith Network for the UK in their document 'Building Good Relations With People of Different Faiths and Beliefs', which appears as Appendix 5, and is widely accepted by both chaplaincies and faith communities, is strongly advocated as a model for inter faith working. Chaplaincies and HEIs are advised to study this guidance as part of any discussion of what constitutes inter faith activity.

For further consideration

Christian chaplaincies have usually regarded themselves as providing a service to the whole HEI that they serve. Providing more specialist support could include recruiting volunteers and paid staff from different faith communities. It will help to consider whether any of the following reasons has led to a chaplaincy remaining exclusively Christian:

- o confidence in the current provision
- o reluctance to change
- o lack of contacts
- o lack of funding
- o resistance from elsewhere.

The resourcing of chaplains and advisors from the world faiths is a significant issue. Initiating and sustaining funding for chaplaincy posts requires informed negotiation with those who have the responsibility for allocating resources. This is true for all faith communities, including the Christian churches, which must justify chaplaincy posts in the light of competing priorities. The difficulties are significant for minority faith groups who both welcome being called on so often to represent themselves at a local and national level, voluntarily and also aspire to find appropriate ways of funding salaried positions for religious professionals to work in the HE sector. New advice and guidance should be drawn up collaboratively about how it may be possible to encourage the resourcing of salaried posts for religious professionals in chaplaincies more often in more places (see 'Conclusions and Next Steps', D5).

A6 Christian chapels per HEI chaplaincy

Number of chapels	Responses
0	50
1	37
2	10
3	3
5	1
9	1

Explanatory note: The question asked was, 'How many sacred spaces are there dedicated or consecrated as Chapels?'

Findings
51% of chaplaincies report at least one chapel dedicated for Christian prayer and worship at the institution(s). 49% report none. This compares to 57% (59) reporting at least one prayer and quiet space and 65% (66) reporting at least one Muslim prayer space. The total number of religious and quiet spaces is 280, an average of 2.75 spaces per chaplaincy

surveyed. Of these spaces, 80 are Christian chapels (29%), 100 are quiet and prayer spaces (36%) and 100 are Muslim prayer rooms (36%). In the institutions visited, surveyed and considered during the project only one HEI synagogue was noted. No mention of any other existing faith specific prayer room apart from Christian Chapels and Muslim prayer rooms was made except in the context of possible future developments.

Recommendations
See below (A10) for 'Recommendations' arising from tables A6 to A10.

For further consideration
See below (A10) for matters 'For further consideration' arising from tables A6 to A10.

A7 Muslim prayer spaces

Number of Muslim prayer spaces	Responses
0	36
1	44
2	12
3	8
4	2

Explanatory note: The question asked was, 'How many permanent prayer spaces are there for the exclusive use of Muslims?'

Findings
Of the 66 chaplaincies that report Muslim prayer rooms, 85% also note generic quiet and prayer spaces and/or Christian chapels. 55% (36) mention Christian chapels, 55% (36) refer to a quiet or prayer space, and 26% (17) report all three types of space. Of the 11% (11) of all survey responses that report Muslim prayer facilities and no other dedicated spaces, six of them also report other temporary religious facilities. There are five chaplaincies that report that the only prayer provision is Muslim and there are no other facilities.

Recommendations
See below (A10) for 'Recommendations' arising from tables A6 to A10.

For further consideration
See below (A10) for matters 'For further consideration' arising from tables A6 to A10.

A8 Permanent spaces for quiet and prayer

Number of Quiet and Prayer spaces	Responses
0	43
1	37
2	14
3	3
4	1
5	3
7	1

Explanatory note: The survey question asked, 'How many other perma-nent spaces are there for quiet and prayer for use by all or some?', so these spaces may be an inter religious space, a quiet space, or other rooms that may have a specific religious purpose. For example, it may be an outdoor peace garden or a room for prayer that would not have been included in the previous two tables because it was not 'dedicated or consecrated' or exclusively for the use of Muslims.

Findings
58% (59) report quiet or prayer rooms. Where such spaces are provided, the majority (63%) report one place, and 37% mention more than one place. This in total is the same number of spaces as Muslim prayer rooms but with a higher average of rooms in fewer locations. Although there are 25% more (100) of these spaces compared with 80 Christian chapels (see tables A6 and A7) the number of chaplaincies who note such spaces is only 9% greater than those with Christian chapels. This is because the average number of quiet and prayer spaces reported is 1.7 compared to 1.6 chapels.

Recommendations
See below (A10) for 'Recommendations' arising from tables A6 to A10.

For further consideration
See below (A10) for matters 'For further consideration' arising from tables A6 to A10.

A9 Types of prayer space provision at HEIs

Types of Provision	Responses
3 types of provision i.e. Christian chapel, Muslim prayer room, prayer and quiet room	**17**
2 types of provision	**49**
Christian chapel, Muslim prayer room only, no prayer and quiet room	*19*
Muslim prayer room, prayer and quiet room, no Christian chapel	*19*
Christian chapel, prayer and quiet room, no Muslim prayer room	*11*
1 type of provision	**28**
Muslim prayer room, no prayer and quiet room, no Christian chapel	*11*
Quiet and prayer room, no Muslim prayer room, no Christian chapel	*12*
Christian chapel no Muslim prayer room, no prayer and quiet room	*5*
0 types of provision except temporary space	**3**
0 types of provision and no temporary space	**5**

Findings
43% (44 chaplaincies) report quiet and prayer facilities as part but not all of the total provision. 46% (47 chaplaincies) report Christian chapels as part but not all of the total provision. 54% (55 chaplaincies) report Muslim prayer rooms as part but not all of the total provision. 65% (66 chaplaincies) report more than one type of permanent space.

Recommendations
See below (A10) for 'Recommendations' arising from tables A6 to A10.

For further consideration
See below (A10) for matters 'For further consideration' arising from tables A6 to A10.

A10 Use of temporary spaces for prayer and worship

	Responses
No use of temporary spaces for prayer and worship	50
Use of temporary spaces for prayer and worship	52

Explanatory note: The question that was asked was 'Are there any temporary spaces used for prayer or worship? Please describe?'

Findings
48% (49) report that temporary facilities at their HEI(s) are accompanied by at least one type of permanent provision. Only three of the chaplaincies report temporary spaces being made available and no dedicated room(s). 18% report at least one type of permanent facility as well as a temporary space, 21% report two other types of permanent facilities in addition to the temporary room and 10% report three other types of permanent facility.

Recommendations (Tables A6-A10)
Chaplaincies report that permanent or temporary physical places for religious observance have been provided in 95% of their HEIs. 64% report at least two different types of place. These actions demonstrate that there is a near total consensus that there should be some provision. Close to a two-thirds majority report two or more types of space. The first practice dialogue (Section B: B1.1-B1.4) provides qualitative evidence about how practitioners are engaging with the issues that are raised. Four narratives (Section C: C1, C4, C6 and C9) all look in depth at the development of new facilities. HEIs should learn from these and other exemplary provisions before opting to create new spaces.

For further consideration (Tables A6–A10)
The relative advantages of having such spaces, and disadvantages of not providing them, cannot be discovered by this brief quantitative research. The narratives and dialogues mentioned above do assist with clarifying what the issues are, and collection of evaluative data on the use of such spaces will be of considerable benefit to those who have already installed such facilities.

Another area for consideration is the sustained use of temporary spaces: over half of the chaplaincies report the use of temporary facilities, and it may well be that timetabled booking of rooms to increase capacity has more advantages than disadvantages. Both these topics merit further discussion.

Although an HEI can express its interest and support for religious observance through the provision of physical facilities, this may be perceived by some of the students and staff with a religious commitment as only a partial response to supporting religious diversity in the institution. Space provision alone stops short of full engagement with diverse needs and practices.

Evidence elsewhere in this report suggests that many people with religious beliefs in an HEI are more likely to discover that their identity is respected and affirmed through having their needs met in relation to:

- o   accommodation and catering
- o   the academic timetable
- o   community celebrations on campus
- o   the exploration of identity through learning opportunities within and beyond the curriculum.

These four things may be more significant for many individuals than the use of a prayer space (see the dialogues B1.1-B1.4).

A11 Diversity of religious student societies

Number of religions represented by student societies	Responses
0	8
1	16
2	19
3	19
4	15
5	7
6	10
7	6
8	1

Explanatory note: This table shows the number of different religions that are represented by student faith societies that are known to the chaplaincy at their HEI.

A12 Number of religious societies known to the chaplaincies

Type of society	Responses
Buddhist	23
Christian	81
Hindu	24
Jewish	40
Muslim	67
Sikh	24
Baha'i	8
Jain	1
Zoroastrian	0
Other religious/belief identity	11

Explanatory note: This table provides a breakdown of the number of student faith societies by religion that are known to chaplaincies at their HEI(s). The category 'other religious/belief identity' refers to any religious or belief view not included in the list of nine faiths (or world religions) presented in the introduction to this report.

Findings
The findings suggest a broad representation of the world religions in student societies. Although this is encouraging, the number of societies identified is typically 50%-60% lower than the numbers listed by national representative groups for faith societies. These groups suggest an even greater representation of world religions in student societies. For instance, websites suggest that, across the UK, the NHSF (National Hindu Students' Forum) has counted a total of 51 Hindu societies, UJS (Union of Jewish Students) more than 100 societies, BOSS (British Organisation of Sikh Students) 46 societies and the Jain Network up to six societies. The research for the present covers only England and Wales and did not count multiple societies in one HEI, neither were duplicate societies counted in the few places where one chaplaincy serves more than one institution, so this may account for some of the difference. Also, sometimes a society may be temporarily inactive. Finally, the survey question was only asked of the responding member of the chaplaincy staff. Consequently the societies present in the HEI that are identified are the ones known to the chaplaincy staff.

Recommendations
Many chaplaincies are fully aware of and supportive of the faith societies of the world religions at their HEI(s). But it is a matter for concern

that there may be a lack of knowledge about faith societies by chaplaincies in HEIs and if there were a difference in knowledge between national coordinating groups and those working in the local context. Liaison between societies and chaplaincies is likely to improve the provision that is made at an HEI for individual students and staff, for faith societies, and for the chaplaincy's strategic planning. Frequent liaison not just between chaplaincies and the societies but also between chaplaincy, Student Services, Students' Union and the individual societies will also assist in ensuring awareness and responsiveness. Increased liaison between the representative national bodies and the chaplaincy networks would be beneficial. Such liaison would improve knowledge, encourage further support of student groups and create the opportunities for collaboration and mutual understanding.

For Further Consideration
As discussed in the seventh Dialogue (B7.2), there are questions to be explored concerning the accessibility of student faith societies, especially in regard to gender, sexuality, race, ethnicity and disability. These factors must be borne in mind carefully when considering how representative a particular society is of the students of a given religion within an HEI.

A13 Non-curricular inter religious activity

	Responses
There are no inter religious student societies	71
There is at least one inter religious student society	31

	Responses
There are no inter religious activities run by the HEI	30
There are inter religious activities run by the HEI	72

Findings
71% report non-curricular inter religious activities and 30% report an inter religious student society. Of the 72 chaplaincies that identify inter religious activities at their HEI(s), 28 have inter religious societies. There are three chaplaincies where the only known inter religious activity occurring in the HEI takes place through the activity of an inter religious society. These results do not provide a measure of the quality of societies or the activities run by the HEI(s). Neither has the level of inter religious activity at HEIs been measured in terms of frequency or

participant numbers. However, data collected suggests some useful examples of inter religious activities, including the inter religious society organizing events at an HEI, a bi-monthly 'faith groups forum', a 'face to faiths' programme where students and staff meet, regular visits to places of worship, a 'centre for religious dialogue' and a 'faith week'.

Recommendations
Considering the encouragements from government, the Equality Challenge Unit, the Inter Faith Network and religious leaders for developing good relations among people of different faiths and beliefs, it is a matter of concern that one in three HEIs do not host any specifically inter religious events to encourage dialogue, and that fewer than one in three HEIs have an inter faith student society. Fostering an environment where this can happen, and facilitating students to develop such dialogue is something to be encouraged. Equality and Diversity teams, Students' Unions, Guilds, Student Services and Chaplaincies can assist in such work. National chaplaincy advisors, Universities UK, GuildHE, the Equality Challenge Unit, the Association of Managers of Student Services in Higher Education (AMOSSHE), the National Union of Students and the Inter Faith Network should help develop good practice guidelines.

For further consideration
A higher education learning environment is an ideal place for deepening understanding of the self and the other. Much learning can and does take place outside of the curriculum. The opportunities for meeting and connecting with people of different perspectives and speaking in depth about matters of both unity and diversity require coordination. Chaplaincies are key to ensuring the creation of such opportunities. It helps when the institution values such learning by generating new funding, allocating and reallocating human resource and encouraging involvement from colleagues including the senior management team. It may be that in the longer term it would be feasible to accredit such learning within a student's personalised curriculum.

A14 Chaplaincies seeking funding

Chaplaincies seeking new funding in the last 5 years	68
Chaplaincies receiving new funding in the last 5 years	56

Explanatory note: The question that was asked was 'Has any new funding been sought for provision for students and staff of faith in the last five years?'

Findings
67% of chaplaincies (68) have sought new funding in the last five years. 68% (46) of them received new money. Eight chaplaincies that sought no new funding did receive some further funding, so in total 53% (54) of chaplaincies have received new funding in the last five years.

Recommendations
The approximate success to failure ratio of 3:1 of those who have sought funding, and the successes in obtaining funding not even applied for in eight instances, indicate that the sector and the faith communities are recognizing the need to assist chaplaincies through funding. Applications are proving to be successful and it is timely for further bids to be put in. This will be particularly important for chaplaincies that want to become effective in providing services that are fit to support a diversity of contemporary religious and belief needs.

For further consideration
When chaplaincies are considering development, or finding that what they are attempting to deliver is unsustainable, it is important to consider the range of funding opportunities available and the potential to collaborate with others to strengthen the bid. For example, a capital project relating to prayer facilities for one faith community presents an ideal opportunity to consider enhancing the project to meet the needs of other communities. In a bid for staff, there is scope for developing roles that have community liaison or employer engagement built-in. If the bid is for research, empowerment of local faith groups through the research activity will strengthen the impact more than one that remains within the academic environment.

A15 Faith/world religion development plans

Explanatory note: The question asked was 'Are there any development plans, targets, protocols or strategic aims for provision for students and staff of faith at the university/college?'

Plans	Responses
Yes	77
No	22
No answer	3

The number of chaplaincies exploring (self-nominated) topics was as follows:

Topics included in plans, targets, protocols and aims	Responses
strategy/policy writing	29
estate	25
faiths	21
staffing	17
inter faith	12
events/societies	9
training/teaching	6
international students	2
timetabling	2
food	1

Findings
75% of chaplaincies (77) know of, or are involved in, strategic planning for provision for faiths at their HEI(s). The most common topics mentioned are writing new strategies and policies, changes to estate and physical space and, staffing. Specific inter religious matters are mentioned less frequently, and issues around faith provision, such as events, timetabling, learning and food feature less frequently still. These results should not be taken as evidence of all that is on the agenda of each chaplaincy or HEI. They do, however, indicate what is being prioritised by those interviewed.

Recommendations
Chaplains are engaged in strategic thinking about a broad range of topics. This suggests a major need and demand for provision of training, support, dialogue and collaboration, both across institutions and also between chaplains and other sections within the HE sector. National advisors, day conference planners, faith communities, funding bodies, training centres and inter religious organisations can all assist with helping chaplains develop their plans. HEIs can help by supporting the training and consultancy needs that will allow staff to be timely and effective in their development planning.

HEIs are far more likely to succeed in improving relations on campus where dialogue, co-operation and collaboration occur. Sophisticated inter religious understanding of a level appropriate to higher education will occur where HEIs (either individually or in partnership) carefully assess and anticipate need and demand and provide accordingly. Equivalence of provision for the religious and belief needs of HEI members must be assessed and acted upon so that institutions are confident their developments are fair, equitable and considerate of the diverse needs and concerns that relate to peoples' religion and belief. It will be critical that any implementation comes after both dialogue and consultation and the outcomes are both transparent and strategic so that those affected are involved throughout the process.

For further consideration
Although questions surrounding provision are being explored, the evidence suggests that grappling with how to develop inter religious co-operation requires further strategic attention. It would appear that there are understandable reasons for a lack of strategic thinking around inter religious issues: simply getting some of the basics in place is being prioritised, including planning, physical spaces and staffing. However, fostering good relations between religions at HEIs is a priority that must shape the strategic work of any chaplaincy that wants to develop its service in way that is timely.

B Practice Dialogues

Explanatory note: The titles of all these dialogues and the questions that follow them are those that were offered for the seven day workshops attended by practitioners. Some of them are deliberately provocative or colloquial or both. These dialogues represent the conversations that took place at the workshops and comments added on the web by practitioners. The 'Findings' in this section reflect the issues and ideas raised by practitioners.

B1 Time and space for faith

B1.1 How does time and space management affect HE chaplains?

Issues, among others, that were considered:

- What is it like for an HE chaplain with or without dedicated physical space?
- Do timetable patterns and opening times substantially affect a chaplaincy?
- Must questions of chaplaincy vision and strategy be time and space led?

Findings
Provision of chaplaincy space that can be used by the institution's members has the benefit of validating those who want to use it by giving them scope to express their religious identity while at the HEI. An under-provision can impede the effective operation of chaplains, particularly when they have little in the way of office space to work from. Chaplaincy work requires office facilities. Many chaplains have models of working that include working outside of an office. Even so, a base that can also serve to welcome people is a minimum requirement.

The timing of the working day and the academic year can overlap with religious celebrations and observances in ways that are challenging and complex. The expansion of the teaching day into the evenings at some HEIs requires a change in response. Providing a responsive service (especially to international students) out of term time creates even more challenges. This is because a significant number of religious festivals may fall outside term time in any calendar year.

Recommendations
HEIs that choose to express their engagement with religion and belief through the built environment need to consider how to respond to the

current diversity of student and staff populations and anticipate future need. Those HEIs that do not have a dedicated chaplaincy facility will benefit from considering the opportunities that there are for other appropriate spaces to be used by student faith societies and chaplaincies for religious observance and celebration.

For further consideration
There are some fascinating examples of chaplains in physically limited or temporary surroundings equipping an environment for worship quite literally from a suitcase. There are many aspects of religious life that are portable, whether they be symbols, prayer mats, or sacred texts. But having to rely on such temporary provision, except in occasional circumstances, may indicate a lesser valuing of religious life and practice by an HEI.

B1.2 Is consistency necessary, or is it more about equivalence?

Issues, among others, that were considered:

- How much of a challenge is developing provision in a reasonably equal way?
- Is non-equivalent funding for provision (external and internal) a problem?
- Is provision affected by gender, sexuality, race, nationality and disability?
- Which approaches effectively encourage good relations and social cohesion?
- How can equivalence be measured for students with differing catering, prayer, timetabling, accommodation and pastoral care requirements?

Findings
Recent guidance on social cohesion and inclusion (Universities UK, GuildHE and the Equality Challenge Unit [2005]) that recommends a tailor-made approach to each distinctive group was mentioned and echoed by practitioners. Where provision is made in terms of time-tabling adjustments or physical spaces, considering an equivalence of provision that reflects the different priorities of different groups is all-important. Student feedback, expert advice, and an overall strategy have all proved to be vital elements in scoping what service level to set for the needs of different religious members of an HEI.

Recommendations

It is important to establish a service users group or groups as part of the process of developing a strategy for reaching an appropriate service level. If there is to be some equivalence in provision for adherents of different religions there must be a sustained level of consultation. A proactive approach such as this is the best way to ensure that some do not feel marginalised, especially when other groups are perceived to be receiving enhanced provision. It may be appropriate and realistic for a religious practitioner from a different strand, tradition or religion to provide pastoral care and signposting to HEI members.

When identifying equivalent levels of service it is essential to recognise that different groups have differing levels of need and aspiration for some of the following

- o social space
- o appropriate living accommodation
- o prayer facilities
- o sacred spaces and places to store religious symbols and writings
- o facilitated opportunities to meet people from their own religion
- o an active interest in the individual
- o a willingness to enter into dialogue
- o an emphasis on the people, not on places.

For further consideration

Developing a service level that comprehends a 'dynamic equivalence' — a level of provision for each religious grouping that translates into something similar for the next without being identical — is a challenge that is yet to be met in nearly every HEI in the UK. HEIs that can model such strategies will gain more than advantage in the sector. They will have ensured that their response relates to identified or anticipated needs rather than being based on assumption. Best provision is that which is designed to be flexible depending on fluctuations in the quantity and requirements of service users.

B1.3 What does dedicated religious space at an HEI signify?

Issues, among others, that were considered:

- ▪ Faiths may have particular facilities at an HEI. What significances might rightly or wrongly be understood by such provision, and by whom?

- Is the most equal space one which everyone can use, or is it better to think of equivalence of provision and meeting diverse needs differently?
- What about provision for New Religious Movements?

Findings
Within one religion there is no singular orthodoxy and so it is unlikely that a single space could be inclusive of all adherents from one faith. Each person using a space will appreciate certain details over others, and each will dislike, like or not care about particular inclusions or omissions. In addition, there are other more practical alterations that affect use of a physical space, including the site's proximity to other facilities, its accessibility and the space's profile and aesthetics.

A further finding is that two reasons why an HEI may want members of different religions to share a facility are:

o   fostering good relations on campus
o   effective space utilisation.

However, some of those wanting to make use of a multi-religious space for prayer or worship may not concur with this and may, for legitimate religious or cultural reasons, prefer dedicated facilities for their own religion.

Thirdly, much of the current HEI provision has happened in a piecemeal and reactive manner. HEIs, typically, have not anticipated need across diverse communities of religious adherents or sought to do so within an overall strategy of providing for religion and belief needs.

Finally, opening or dedicating a facility can denote it as a sacred space in a number of religions. This means that the facility may come to be regarded quite differently by HEI senior managers, its custodians (frequently the chaplaincy), and those who use it.

Recommendations
HEIs that have Christian spaces are likely to have established them in the last two hundred years but not in the last few years. HEIs that have inter religious prayer rooms, quiet spaces and Muslim prayer spaces have usually opened these in the last few years.

When considering issues of equivalence between religions it is essential to:

o   take into consideration the numbers of adherents
o   consult on need

o involve service users and local faith communities at every stage of developing a strategy

o involve service users in determining the provision of facilities.

For further consideration
The highly valued independence of each HEI must not result in a barrier to some collective consideration in the sector of appropriate future provision. Inter-institutional dialogue on this topic will be the best guarantee against ill thought-out imitation of existing provisions. There is a risk that any particular institution's model will be perceived as best practice because it exists and is seen to work well. However, the model may simply reflect a particular context at a particular point of the institution's development.

Achieving consensus on appropriate and equivalent provision is a challenge that is assisted by the world religions' recognition of each other as partners in inter faith dialogue. However those with other religious or belief perspectives are not involved in conversations with all the faith communities at the level of inter faith dialogue. This means achieving a consensus between *all* religious and belief perspectives about space provisions is unrealistic. Advice and guidance on how HEIs should respond to diverse religious and belief needs must therefore be prioritised (see 'Conclusions and Next Steps D5).

B1.4 Festivals and Holy Days: conundrums or times to celebrate?

Issues, among others, that were considered:

- Are festivals and holy days more likely to be seen as a timetabling conundrum or an opportunity for celebrations in the HE setting?
- How can the HEI pick and choose which festivals it celebrates?
- What steps lead to successful religious celebrations in the HEI?

Findings
Chaplaincies that make full provision for the faiths find that for all faiths festival celebrations and holy day observances are as important (or more important) than provision of physical space for such events or for prayer and worship. Students and staff who find that their own religion is acknowledged can feel as affirmed as another faith adherent does by having a place to go and pray in.

Areas that have been shown to have a significant impact include:

- o   community celebrations at an HEI
- o   creating scheduled opportunities for students and staff to participate in local community observances and festivals
- o   adjusting the academic timetable in a way that is considerate of diverse religious and belief needs.

Recommendations

All chaplaincies need to reflect on the excellent practice that has been developed by those that are leaders in this field. Strategic planning and time and space needs, when considered in tandem, are likely to lead to a reasonable and suitable level of provision that is both fit for purpose, sustainable and flexible. Other more piecemeal approaches are to be discouraged.

For further consideration

There are some excellent examples of faith community celebrations at HEIs within the UK sector (see the practice narratives in Section C of this chapter). Development of best practice will come from engaging leaders from the faith communities with a brief for HE issues. Listening to the faith communities will help those planning at a national level, particularly the Higher Education Funding Council Executive, Universities UK, and GuildHE. This listening should occur alongside a consultative dialogue with chaplaincies, the Association of Managers of Student Services in Higher Education (AMOSSHE), National Union of Students, Equality Challenge Unit and the Inter Faith Network, and HEI senior management teams.

B2 Faith volunteers and HE chaplaincy

Explanatory note: This dialogue's principal focus was on the value of the contribution that volunteers bring to chaplaincies (see, for example, B2.4). This dialogue did not explore in any depth the increased resourcing of salaried appointments for religious professionals from the world faiths. This is addressed earlier in this chapter in A5 'For further consideration' and also in 'Conclusions and Next Steps' D5.

B2.1 How important is the faith volunteer in the HEI?

Issues, among others, that were considered:

- What are the reasons that a chaplaincy may depend on volunteers?
- Where are the volunteers being found to work in HE chaplaincies?
- How is the generosity of faith volunteering valued by the HEI?
- How dependent are inter faith relationships on voluntary time giving?

Findings
Many of the new staff joining chaplaincy teams in HEIs are volunteers. One of the growing number of responsibilities for existing salaried team members is to help to manage and coordinate a larger team. Many Christian and Jewish chaplaincy posts are funded, in part or totally, by their faith communities. To date there has been very little funding for chaplaincy by other faith communities. Volunteers from faith communities have a significant role to play in ensuring that various faiths are represented within chaplaincies. Volunteering makes it more feasible to ensure representation from different strands or traditions from within one religion without it becoming too costly. It also prevents the situation arising that only those faith groups who can fund posts are able to be involved in chaplaincy teams. It may be practical for a volunteer to come and give an educational seminar on an occasional basis and in doing so ensure that awareness is raised about particular strands, traditions or religious minorities. For all these reasons volunteering is seen by practitioners as a valuable part of chaplaincy activity.

Recommendations
If an HEI chaplaincy is to serve the diverse religious and belief needs of students and staff, it will benefit from having staff from faith

communities that are represented within the institution and/or locally. These staff can, at least, provide a point of contact. Above and beyond that, enthusiastic team members may choose to offer to be involved in an even more substantial way. This is to be welcomed where appropriate levels of support, leadership and contractual agreements are made. There is a challenge in determining whose offers of voluntary help to accept, so as to develop best practice both in expanding the volunteer team and selecting suitable people for posts. Ensuring that volunteers will help see that the needs of diverse groups within a religion are catered for should be a priority in recruiting appropriate staff.

For further consideration
Engaging only those faith communities that are members of a local inter faith forum (or at least a local forum or council within a specific faith community) allows the HEI or chaplaincy to work within parameters that are already set at a local level rather than devising new ones. This way, those who are nominated to volunteer are known to be coming from a context that is supportive of collaborative practice. It is also important to consider which volunteers will be working with vulnerable adults and under 19s. All may need to have CRB checks. Although the development of inter faith teams in chaplaincies will typically depend on volunteering in the short term, consideration should be given as to whether further funding can be drawn down to secure the roles of faith advisors and chaplains.

B2.2 Building equality in a team: who's supporting whom?

Issues, among others, that were considered:

- How do chaplaincies ensure that all team members feel valued and included when members are differently motivated, funded and accredited?
- What do faith volunteers embody by being both giver and worker?
- How are faith volunteers perceived by their own local faith community?
- What are the strengths and weaknesses of line-management occurring within or beyond the team (e.g. lead chaplain or director of Student Services)?
- What about gender, sexuality and disability issues in relation to volunteers?

Findings
Leaders and managers of teams committed to treating all team members as equals recognise that there are inequalities in the provision for volunteers:

- o   terms and conditions of their employment fluctuate
- o   space available for them is variable
- o   there can be role tension between the sending group or community and the task within a chaplaincy team

Those in team leadership also recognised how challenging it is to lead and manage a diverse team of staff effectively. There is an expressed need for further training and sharing of exemplary practice.

Recommendations
Critical issues relating to building team equality will always include ensuring appropriate parity of treatment between voluntary and salaried staff. However, practitioners have identified that even more important is the model of group working that is developed. A commitment to team working through collaboration and liaison accompanied by parity of esteem is more important than whether staff are voluntary or salaried.

For further consideration
Any consideration of equality within a team must also take into account how team members will serve their constituency with equality. People accessing the chaplaincy service must be guaranteed a non-discriminatory service. That requires the drawing up of working agreements that allow individuals to exercise their personal conscience in a manner that does not prevent a student obtaining appropriate support. If a difference of belief leads to a team member being unable to offer suitable support, then there is always the principle of cross-referral that allows a guaranteed level of support from the service.

B2.3 What rights and responsibilities for the faith volunteer?

Issues, among others, that were considered:

- ▪   What aspirations is it wise for the volunteer, team leader and institution to have about such a role?
- ▪   What is helpful to include in job descriptions and contracts?
- ▪   What is helpful to include in partnership agreements with external groups?

Findings
Local faith groups may offer to a chaplaincy their own nomination for appointment and this can be challenging, especially if there is a difference in expectations between the individual, the sending organisation and the chaplaincy. Ensuring that volunteers are included and consulted requires effective communications strategies. Clear partnership agreements with external groups means volunteers serve in a representative way, making it simpler to find replacements when a volunteer leaves.

Recommendations
Chaplaincies that are staffed to any extent by volunteers will benefit from drawing up agreed terms and conditions of working with volunteers. It will be useful to include some guidelines or principles on inter faith collaboration and co-operation. For instance, some volunteers may work in a chaplaincy to serve people from their own faith background. Other volunteers will assist all those who have a need. Clarifying from the outset what is and is not expected is important, as is ensuring that expenses, training, facilities and communications are all clearly understood by the volunteers in order to ensure an efficient, structured and inclusive working environment.

For further consideration
There are challenges in finding a willing volunteer who is representative of a local faith community and who is appreciated and endorsed by the students and staff of that faith in the HEI. There may be many multiple strands or traditions within a faith community and different systems of authority and accountability. Therefore, where there is a desire to develop a coherent inter religious chaplaincy service, it is necessary to translate differences in a way that both looks equal from the outside and feels equal for those staff who belong to the team.

B2.4 Faith volunteering: both a solution and a catalyst for funding?

Issues, among others, that were considered:

- Is the status quo of having some volunteers and some salaried staff adequate?
- How can volunteering catalyse funding?
- Are there only advantages to seeking local funding to develop roles?

Findings

Volunteering is itself a form of resourcing, which although a gift from the individual and his or her faith community, has a substantial value and natural flexibility. Voluntary work allows the growth of a service, without having to depend on larger contributions from existing funding streams or expanding the sources of income for a chaplaincy. Participation in the life of an HEI, and having the opportunity to give something back to the local community or institution, can be an appropriate incentive, especially for those who are offering to do a small number of hours per week. There are examples of volunteering that could serve as a catalyst for further funding.

Recommendations

Volunteers are to be valued as a resource in their own right. A faith community can become highly successful in participating in HE chaplaincy through encouraging and supporting volunteers to participate. This has fewer economic implications and allows those groups that have previously been marginalised to participate in collaborative teams. It may well be that such activity will serve as a catalyst for funding though this need not be seen as an end goal.

For further consideration

Highly experienced people who are representative of a faith community may have more of an incentive to find a voluntary chaplaincy role, where there is a greater opportunity to work in a flexible way, than to seek paid employment. It may well be that those who volunteer already work part or full time and others may be retired. Designing a team model that seeks to use volunteers may have many more advantages over seeking funding first to pay for posts.

B3 The Christian chaplain as theologian in an HE inter faith context

Explanatory note: This workshop was advertised without 'Christian' in the title. However, when only Christians confirmed attendance at the day, it was deemed appropriate not to require them to speak for theologies other than their own, and so the title was amended. This created a space for Christians to address their theology in relation to their work with and alongside others in more diverse teams. This was a suitable topic for one of seven dialogues because Christian chaplains have a large responsibility in leading inter religious teams, since in nearly every instance, it is a Christian who is in such a position. The conversation explored how Christian leadership within chaplaincies is expressed in a varied and complex landscape of chaplaincy and HE. Another Practice Dialogue (B6) explored an inter faith ethic for working collaboratively in.chaplaincy.

B3.1 Setting the scene: the Christian chaplain in the HE context

Issues, among others, that were considered:

- What has been the distinctive role of Christian chaplains in HEIs?
- What are the theological underpinnings for Christian chaplaincy in HE?
- How are the tensions felt by Christian chaplains between: church and institution; pastoral care and mission; evangelism and student support; inter faith and equal opportunities?

Findings

Many models of chaplaincy exist and their shape depends on:

- the HEI context
- the person leading the team
- the support from the faith communities
- the tasks undertaken on behalf of the HEI
- the physical space that is allocated for chaplaincy use
- the level of engagement in governance and management
- whether there is collaborative inter religious working.

All these factors will influence the development of a theology (and/or philosophy) that undergirds a chaplaincy. It is because there is such a diversity of approaches that a theology of chaplaincy needs to be articulated. Although this is something that many have tried, some successfully, each new circumstance requires a new articulation of theology.

The ecology of responsibilities between chaplaincies and others within the HEI, and the interaction between religious groups and individuals, may lead to layers of complexity that confound those attempting to reflect theologically on practice.

Recommendations
Theological and philosophical reflection on practice allows those working in chaplaincy to infuse their models of working with an ethic that is not simply driven by institutional operational standards. This benefits the chaplaincy service and helps facilitate change within the HEI. It also protects chaplaincy from having only a brokering role only when inter- and intra-religious tensions arise.

For further consideration
How the HEI is understood will vary dependant on whose perspective is being articulated. Those within chaplaincy carry some authority when attempting to express an understanding of the nature of religious practice within the HEI and of religious perceptions of the institution. Within a post-modern and post-Christian context, such interpretations are valuable to those who are shaping institutional mission and vision (see Section B4.1-B4.4 for a further discussion of this).

B3.2 The Chaplain as Theologian

Issues, among others, that were considered:

- What might a Christian theology of chaplaincy look like amid the challenges of working in a 'multi-faith' context?

Findings
A Christian theology of chaplaincy is more clearly shaped when those working in chaplaincy are clear about the place they inhabit, so that their reflection is contextualised. It also is important that in the shaping of a theology, there is some clarity about the people and places in which such a theology will be expressed. The British democratic context has a very different settlement between secular and religious life compared with the somewhat parallel democratic structures of France and the United States. In Britain there is an opportunity within the public forum to allow a greater divergence of opinion, and therefore a fuller expression of theology, than in other nations where religion is separated off from secular life. This means that chaplaincies can help

religious expression to be shared in a format that is understandable to a variety of groupings within the institution.

Recommendations
Raising questions of meaning and purpose is part of the work of chaplaincy (see Tim Jenkins [2006]). This is a route to working out a theology for chaplaincy and, in fact, a theological route for reflecting on HE culture, too. Chaplaincy can be an experiment in discernment of institutional life, where inter religious hospitality can be expressed and tested. Scriptural reasoning (see below) between different faith groups can deepen understanding. Chaplaincy can serve an HEI well as a location for appropriate:

- o   mutual hospitality between faiths
- o   religious discussion and argument
- o   inter religious collaboration
- o   the celebration of the divine and human spirituality.

For further consideration
If there is to be a fuller articulation of a theology of chaplaincy then the principles of contextual theology and collaborative writing and peer review could all assist. This will help to gather theologies together that relate to the variety of contexts where HE chaplaincy work is undertaken.

B3.3 Theological reflections on coordinating 'multi-faith' teams.

Issues, among others, that were considered:

- ▪   Christian chaplains are, in the vast majority of cases, the team leaders or coordinators of teams representing several world religions (and occasionally New Religious Movements too). What are the theological challenges for service, oversight, collaboration and management?

Findings
Leadership and collaboration are building blocks for successful team development. Because of this, they serve as constituent parts of what makes up a theology of coordinating a chaplaincy. Further materials that can be used as resources are those of commonality and difference. Theological agendas within a team will differ, and sometimes overlap.

Recommendations
Two differing models of inter religious working are:

- o developing a framework for co-operation between diverse peoples where each identity is valued and celebrated
- o having neutral ground where the individual must diminish the self to enter a shared space.

The former is focused on collaboration, the latter on tolerance. The latter is about the lessening of the self, so as to accommodate the other. The former is about allowing each member to be at their fullest when collaborating with the other, and therefore represents a more holistic approach. To achieve mutuality, work by consensus will be required. Thus an inductive rather than a deductive model of working is likely to be more successful in shaping the context of a specific team in a particular environment.

For further consideration
Increasingly, the practice of 'scriptural reasoning' is being used to deepen mutual understanding and collaborative practice between faiths in a number of settings, including the HE sector. Scriptural reasoning gives the opportunity for faith adherents to share and discuss the meaning of their scriptures in relation to the meanings contained in the scriptures of other faith adherents who are also present. This enables the construction of new meanings of identity and theology through mutuality. Adventuring into such territory, though, depends on building relationships, over time.

B3.4 Who can map the currents in theology and HE chaplaincy?

Issues, among others, that were considered:

- How do currents in theology impact on approaches to Christian inter faith chaplaincy team leadership?
- How do shifts in theological thinking help or hinder mapping a theology of ministry?
- May the ministry of HE chaplains influence developments in a theology of ministry?

Findings
Chaplains, by being part of the 'church in the world', can certainly be part of the process of assessing currents in theology, in the way they as practitioners influence patterns of theology and ministry in HE chaplaincy. In fact, sector ministries including HE chaplaincy, are influencing models of ministry within different denominations. The chaplain can also assist the academics and students to interconnect their disciplines to faith. Ethics is an important key and can serve as a focus

around which a common discourse can develop. One chaplaincy has set up a curriculum group to look at how issues of diversity impact on curriculum development.

Recommendations

There is an opportunity within the HE setting to 'speak truth to power' (see Stephen Sykes [2006]). This is the case both within an HEI, and true of the HEI itself. Within an HEI, those holding some distinctive interpretations of human identity and common values, including chaplains, can articulate those ideas to people who hold power, so that their perspectives may have a positive influence, for instance, on an institution's ethics or cohesiveness. This will be most effective when diverse interpreters of truth collaborate to express their shared concerns to those in authority within the HEI. At the same time the discernment of truth, albeit partial, is central to academic enquiry and yet Gordon Graham (2005) has written on the inability of British universities to speak truth to power. This, too is potentially an activity that chaplaincy can facilitate.

For further consideration

There are strands within the diverse belief systems in British society that do not want to seek mutuality or consensus, and herein lies a further challenge to a Rawlsian model of overlapping consensus and political toleration. Again, chaplaincies are well placed to serve as points of meeting (even for those who, under many circumstances, may not wish to enter into dialogue). It may be that establishing such places, combined with the building of trust, will enable individuals to choose to join a conversation that will confront their own identity. This may also lead to the moderation of less accommodating modes of thought. This is explored further in the Dialogues B6.1-B6.4 (Section B).

B4 HEI mission and vision

B4.1 Where might religion and belief fit with institutional aims?

Issues, among others, that were considered:

- Where does religion and belief impinge on the HEI beyond the curriculum?
- Is it appropriate for an HEI's key aims to relate to spirituality and faith?
- What role might a chaplaincy have in developing institutional vision?
- What is changing about funding streams for religious provision?

Findings
An HEI's chaplaincy can make a significant contribution to the way an institution is able to construct a clear narrative about itself, develop an ethos, and choose an orientation towards religion and belief issues. Chaplaincy practitioners know that they are assisting in meeting an HEI's aims around widening participation, social cohesion and community partnership, and realise that gaining a better recognition of this (perhaps by articulating it more clearly) would be helpful.

Recommendations
HEIs should naturally progress from setting their Key Performance Indicators to using them to intersect positively with religion and belief issues. A second aspiration an HEI should have is to ensure that chaplaincy activity is written into relevant strategic plans and service levels. This requires the championing of the work, both by the chaplaincy among senior staff and by senior staff too. Chaplains and heads of Student Services identified that a clearer articulation of the work that chaplaincies undertake is necessary. When this happens, further funding for chaplaincy is more likely to follow.

For further consideration
Chaplaincies help engage students where race, religion, ethnicity and culture overlap. Chaplaincies face a further task of seeking to ensure the inclusion of those whose sexuality, gender, disability and social background as well as religion and belief may lessen their ability to express their identity within the social, cultural and academic aspects of a higher education setting.

B4.2 How do chaplaincies and cultural inclusion agendas intersect?

Issues, among others, that were considered:

- What value is there in celebrating cultural and religious festivals at the HEI?
- Do 'widening participation', 'equality and diversity', and 'internationalisation' agendas influence chaplaincy development and vice versa?
- To what extent should non-curricular faith issues reside with chaplaincy?
- What key performance indicators can be identified for HEIs developing strategies that address the religion and belief needs of students and staff?

Findings

Most religious professionals working at HEIs are familiar with having a management responsibility for religious diversity. Such a role has its challenges. Some chaplains view it positively as an opportunity for hospitality and leading the way in ensuring that all are included. Most chaplaincies play a role in encouraging celebration of cultural and religious diversity. Some chaplains are troubled by such a role, not wanting to be placed in a position of patronage above those of different faiths. Others are unsettled by being put in the position of a figure-head for a range of different religions within the life of an HEI.

Recommendations

Chaplaincies are frequently at the leading edge of relationship-building between culturally and religiously diverse groups of people. Their knowledge and expertise about aspects of the HEI's life can be very helpful — for instance in advising on how an institution welcomes students. When an HEI is setting Key Performance Indicators that intersect with religion and belief issues, consulting the chaplaincy to identify where progress is most needed, could help HEIs assess needs more accurately.

For further consideration

HEIs can support and encourage students and staff to express their identities by organizing events themselves. This secures the position of the chaplain as supporter and friend rather than gatekeeper. Phrases to consider applying to the role of chaplain may include 'gatekeeper' or 'champion' for cultural and religious inclusion (which some practitioners viewed negatively). This does not require the chaplains to be the representatives of a belief system other than their own. What it does mean is extolling the positive actions of others who have over-lapping agendas.

B4.3 When do HEIs develop Mission and Vision distinctively?

Issues, among others, that were considered:

- Does an institution's foundation and size affect mission and vision?
- What makes a hospitable HEI environment for religious students and staff?
- In what ways do Church HEIs lead and lag in relation to faith provision?
- Is it the social cohesion agenda and faith affiliations that provide the main drivers for placing religion and belief into HEI strategic aims?

Findings
Some HEIs have been motivated by social inclusion agendas to develop their strategic aims in relation to religion and belief issues. Other HEIs have been motivated to develop their response to religion and belief matters because of the recruitment of international students. Many HEIs have been motivated by both these factors. The inclusion of religion and belief matters when developing internationalisation and widening participation agendas as part of an HEI's mission and vision requires confidence and experience in this specific area of equalities concerns and a commitment by the senior management team.

Recommendations
Training of leaders, governors and managers in HEIs on religion and belief issues will help institutions to develop distinctive contributions. Such approaches tend to be more successful where senior staff and chaplaincies engage creatively together in developing mission and vision in relation to religion and belief.

Chaplaincies that seek both to learn from and involve people who represent diverse communities make a valued contribution to the over-all institution. They can assist an HEI in considering how to shape its mission and vision in a manner that relates to all students and staff, whatever their religious or belief commitments.

For further consideration
Church HEIs have tended to be attentive to matters of Christian prac-tice in relation to institutional identity. This emphasis on a particular

set of religious values does not automatically ensure that a Church HEI's mission prioritises religious freedoms; but it will go a long way to doing so if values are expressed in terms of a commitment to the search for truth, which in turn requires that there is a commitment to support people's individual freedoms, including to express their particular faith or belief. Some Church foundation HEIs have, at times, underplayed their religious identity when attempting to market the institution, and so sought other ways to define their distinctiveness. But engaging with faiths and seeking to be inclusive of difference will assist an HEI to prove itself welcoming and hospitable to a diverse range of students and staff.

B4.4 Spiritual maturation and the HEI: whose responsibility?

Issues, among others, that were considered:

- What strategies can be developed for fostering spiritual maturity in an HEI?
- When may religion and belief issues restrict HEI mission and vision?
- How can religious and belief needs add value in an HEI?
- What can be done to help people tap the creative resource of spirituality?

Findings
Questions of religion, belief, spiritual and moral development interrelate with health and wellbeing agendas. Where those in leadership, governance and management of an HEI lack expertise in religion and belief issues, such topics may be more likely to be conceptualised as a problem and threat, rather than as an opportunity and challenge. Developing spiritual maturity in an HEI requires the institution to go beyond having voluntary student and staff groups of like-minded people sustaining their beliefs through societies and meetings. Rather, the HEI, normally through the chaplaincy, and sometimes through the Equality and Diversity department, moves towards dialogue and mutual respect within difference.

Recommendations
Spiritual and religious difference, when successfully explored at an HEI through dialogue, interaction and collaboration (such as joint events or celebrations), leads to a deepening inter religious understanding within institutional life. This can result in greater understanding between individuals of particular faiths. An HEI that prioritises inter religious

activity and dialogue encourages a mature identity by fostering understanding and the respectful exchange of diverse, even conflicting, ideas.

For further consideration
HEIs with thriving single faith societies and yet no inter religious activities are likely to find that diverse viewpoints are reinforced without
any deepening relationships between different groupings within the
institution. Promoting good relations and fostering social cohesion will
require the facilitation of substantial dialogue as well as supporting all
faiths.

B5 Faith communities as HEI stakeholders

B5.1 Are some more welcome than others?

Issues, among others, that were considered:

- How can the doorway into an HEI be designed to offer a clear welcome to current and prospective students and staff from faith communities?
- How might an HEI inadvertently send unwelcoming messages to faiths?
- How can faith communities help HEIs develop the social inclusion agenda?
- How can faiths support curriculum development that reflects local diversity?

Findings
On entering an HEI as a new student or staff member, those who are religious are likely to experience varying levels of hospitality. Chaplaincies are well aware of this. Getting the welcome right for new students and giving clear signals to prospective students can have a positive impact both on recruitment and retention from socially, culturally, ethnically and internationally diverse communities. Drawing a more varied community into an HEI can provide the impetus for new developments in curriculum and for fresh community engagement.

Recommendations
HEIs should consider offering students the option, at registration, to voluntarily identify their religion. This will give HEIs a head start in scoping the religious and belief provision that is appropriate to their student profile. There are concerns about asking for this information; however, the opportunity to share it voluntarily may benefit both the student and the institution and help foster trust. When a student is given an option of sharing their religious identity information, an accompanying statement may help. The HEI can explain its valuing of religious identity and its commitment to keep all details confidential.

This is a student-centred approach to helping to guide service provision that will help with evaluative reporting and a fuller analysis of student satisfaction. This has already occurred in a number of HEIs. National chaplaincy advisors, Universities UK, GuildHE, the Equality Challenge Unit, the Association of Managers of Student Services in Higher Education (AMOSSHE), National Union of Students and the

Inter Faith Network should help develop good practice guidelines for creating the option for such information to be shared.

Having an inter religious chaplaincy and an inter faith forum where common concerns are shared can also help. Publicity about the academic timetable, catering and housing in order to accommodate religious needs was noted as being significant in getting the welcome right.

For further consideration
The relationship that forms when an HEI and local faith communities provide for the religion and belief needs of students and staff can lead to:

  o   collaborative working
  o   new funding streams
  o   the avoidance of unnecessary duplication of activity
  o   HEI participation in strengthening social cohesion
  o   increased opportunities for the HEI to widen participation.

B5.2 What place for both competition and bridge building in the HE religious market place?

Issues, among others, that were considered:

  ▪   Can an HE religious professional hold the tension between the conflicting roles of advocate, salesperson and reconciler?
  ▪   Can faith representatives working at or for an HEI benefit from collaborative working while seeking to promote their religions' distinctive outlooks?

Findings
Recognizing difference and promoting harmony is an essential task for chaplaincies. This can begin within a chaplaincy team itself. Where there is a diverse representation within the chaplaincy team, members have more opportunity to express their distinctive identities. This does not prevent chaplaincy staff from supporting students and colleagues who have different belief positions to their own. Rather, it enables chaplaincy staff to become experts at engaging with difference and relating to diverse needs. Diversity within a team can also enable members to have a fuller appreciation of the varied approaches to religious expression contained not only within the strands and traditions of their own faith but also within other faith communities too.

Recommendations
Working together from diverse starting points can be profoundly creative and promotes community cohesion at a deep level. It can also lead to greater confidence in cross-referral and new approaches to collaboration at regional and national level also.

Chaplaincies with a number of religions represented within a collaborative team will benefit from encouraging substantial discussion of difference and diversity as well as equality and commonality. In fact, this is one of the strengths of an inter faith team. Each member of the team has greater opportunity to express what is different about their own approach, rather than always seeking to deliver the overall common services of the chaplaincy.

For further consideration
A chaplaincy can serve, with the HEI, as an advocate for people of faith. Such advocacy, however, can be a challenging and sensitive matter that needs working through with due care and consideration. First, while a chaplaincy may seek to ensure that HEI rules and regulations are written to ensure standards include religion and belief issues, this may be a complex and slow task. Secondly, a chaplaincy can help faith adherents in understanding how much difference there is within religious practice in their own religion. This can help reduce religious and inter religious conflict by reducing tensions through painstaking interpretation of beliefs.

B5.3 Faith provision and internationalisation

Issues, among others, that were considered:

- Can an HEI treat international students equally, or similarly?
- To ensure equality must faith be 'edited out' or 'vigorously included'?

Findings
Many international students who arrive at British HEIs come from cultures where religion is something that is central both to their personal identity and their culture. Many HEIs are recognizing the need to support and enable students and staff to express their identity in ways that include their religion(s) and culture(s). It is important that HEIs should be prepared and equipped to respond to need and demand, and to manage the expectations of international students. Promotion of an HEI to prospective international students may well place a greater

level of emphasis on provision for religious and belief needs than in home based materials.

Recommendations
It is important to ensure that HEI marketing materials aimed at international students accurately describe how a student can express their religious identity at the receiving institution. Chaplaincies are well placed to provide appropriate advice on this. They can help to collate information on the local faith communities and provision within the HEI itself in a manner that is accurate and balanced. This will help a prospective student to be realistic about what it will be like both on arrival and during their time at the institution.

For further consideration
Some religion and belief provision at an HEI may have been put in place as part of its programme of adjustments to accommodate international students. It will also be helpful to consider questions of equivalence when determining provision for different religions and beliefs, and when encouraging holistic personal development for all HEI members.

B5.4 What place for religion in the HEI?

Issues, among others, that were considered:

- How can religious student societies sit within student democracies?
- What difference would it make for the HEI to see faiths as stakeholders?

Findings
Most Students' Unions successfully accommodate student faith groups within their portfolio of societies. However, there can be occasions where there are misunderstandings. For example, what may appear as an unnecessary replication of societies to some may in fact be the result of different groups seeking to meet different needs. Another more challenging issue is that views commonly held within a faith society on sexuality, gender and religious practice may not be representative of the diverse perspectives expressed within the faith the society is part of. The 'Conclusions and Next Steps' section of this report stresses the need for prompt guidance to be drawn up on this matter (D5). In terms of faith societies sitting within student democratic frameworks, this is entirely possible, especially if the aims of the society require the elected officers to fulfil the religious purpose of the society. Similarly many HEIs are finding that there are many ways of interacting with local

faith communities — not just through renting their premises, but also in local community engagement, hosting public celebrations, inviting faith leaders to sit on relevant committees and organizing visits and volunteering within the local contexts.

Recommendations
Student faith societies and local faith communities can transform the identity and culture of an HEI when they are valued and included by the institution. Both societies and local faith groups serve as points of contact and gathering, and enable the exchange of news and ideas. HEIs that do engage in formal and informal ways are enriched and more able to assist in unlocking potential among those who want to work together for reasons of religion and belief.

For further consideration
Local faith communities can be effective stakeholders in an HEI's life. One way in which they may help is by serving as a moderating influence upon relevant student faith societies. For a society to receive appropriate support from a local faith community's learned wisdom requires careful relational building, the benefits being stability and connectivity. Good community links can assist in the recruitment of local students and staff.

B6 An inter faith ethic for HE chaplaincy

Explanatory note: This title was given in a deliberately ambiguous way in order to stimulate dialogue, rather than to suggest that there is in fact a defining ethic. The title could be about ethics and inter faith or a chaplaincy ethic on inter faith working or both. The title does serve as a route to encourage the exploration of the following issues:

- o developing a general ethical code
- o guidelines for handling inter religious issues
- o guidelines for the appropriate encouragement of inter faith dialogue in appropriate ways.

All of matters are the responsibility of the HEI itself and not just of the chaplaincy.

B6.1 What ethical issues do inter faith chaplaincies face?

Issues, among others, that were considered:

- ▪ How may an ethical code for chaplaincy be decided?
- ▪ What might an ethical code for chaplaincy look like?
- ▪ Are the ethics of good relations on campus problematic?
- ▪ When does chaplaincy challenge HE ethics?

Findings

There are a number of ethical challenges for chaplaincies engaged in inter faith working. First, there are the differing ethics of team members, for example in relation to sexual ethics; however, this variety can be advantageous since it can enable a greater ability to respond to the varied perspectives shared by the people who come to use the service. Secondly, there is a need to shape appropriate codes of conduct by members of the chaplaincy team. The ethics of chaplaincies having management responsibility for religious diversity varies from institution to institution. The following principles were identified as constituent parts of what may shape a chaplaincy's ethic:

- o affirmation of identity
- o freedom from discrimination
- o attention to religious holidays
- o prayer space
- o engaging with humanism and secularism
- o engaging with HEI ethical issues.

Recommendations

Who may be a member of staff in a chaplaincy and who may be supported by a chaplaincy is a matter that depends on the authority that the chaplaincy comes under. Different traditions will have different criteria. Ascertaining what ethical perspectives team members have (and the religious authorities they are accountable to) especially on matters of inter religious co-operation is important. A significant issue that may occur is in relation to working with New Religious Movements. Consideration at a local and national level should be given to developing an ethic that determines what religious activities it is appropriate to include and exclude from HEIs. This ethic will need to determine how boundaries are set and by whom. Developing a code must involve national chaplaincy advisors, Universities UK, the Equality Challenge Unit, the Association of Managers of Student Services in Higher Education (AMOSSHE), National Union of Students and the Inter Faith Network, so that contents for an HEI specific code are identified.

For further consideration

First, to engage with contrasting perspectives requires substantial skill. Chaplaincies will be wise to engage with experts on the diverse strands and traditions within a faith community rather than relying on advocates for just one particular perspective. Those appointing staff to a chaplaincy must bear this in mind. The challenges of inter religious collaboration include being able to manage intra-faith and inter faith tensions around ethics. Secondly, mainstream religious identity and practice is likely, at times, to be in contradiction to the ethics and practices within an HEI. Such issues arise in relation to:

- o   observing holy times and days
- o   the sale of food and drink prohibited within a religion
- o   research ethics that are at a variance with certain belief systems.

The role tension this creates for chaplaincy team members must be taken into consideration by staff at the HEIs they work in.

B6.2 Religious stallholders in the ideologies market place?

Issues, among others, that were considered:

- •   Can free-market economics inform HE spiritual provision?
- •   Do 'diversity' and 'common good' agendas conflict?

- Do 'world religions' have first call on chaplaincy services?
- When does self-promotion become competitive proselytism?

Findings

Proselytism (seeking to convert others to one's own faith) and self-promotion are activities at the heart of several religions, and it need not be problematic for people in an HEI setting to promote their religion to others in the hope that more people will become faith adherents. Invitation events are a particular example of a way a faith society can promote itself in an acceptable way. Student societies that want to educate others about their faith, engender respect and encourage membership can successfully organise events that do not offend the sensibilities of others and need not come into conflict with HEI policy.

Inter faith dialogue enables students to understand more of their own and other faiths. However, the disparity between funding spent on chaplaincy staff and space provision for different communities can cause tensions which are a barrier to dialogue. Also, with 'free market' sponsorship there comes a risk of undue influence over the shape of a chaplaincy.. Those who contribute external funding are more likely to secure facilities or staffing that meet their own interests. The influence of external funders also contains the inherent risk of competitive marketing of religious identities, and therefore external funding needs to be given and accepted with due regard to the due protocols both of the faith community and the HEI.

Recommendations

Setting service level agreements is appropriate whether the chaplaincy is within or adjacent to the HEI. This brings a greater clarity about what is and is not being provided by the chaplaincy. In addition, when the chaplaincy is transparent about the way in which it is financed there is a better chance that no misunderstandings will occur about how a chaplaincy is shaped in relation to its funding.

Chaplaincies can help in facilitating inter faith dialogue and debate. This can be beneficial in allowing those who want energetically to communicate about their own faith to meet similarly energised people from different faiths and traditions. Learning how to engage in complex argument is part of what higher education aspires to achieve among its members. It also increases mutual understanding and there is plenty of scope for inter religious debate within an HEI setting. This is a journey that, if made, is likely to deepen understanding and respect for all who participate appropriately.

For further consideration

Chaplaincy team leaders can become brokers for faiths other than their own within the HEI setting. In nearly every instance, though, they have a religious commitment themselves. It is important to construct a team model that liberates each member, including the team leader, so that they can express their own religious perspective and identity. To ask the team leader to speak on behalf of the chaplaincy is fine, but speaking only in generic terms diminishes the specialist skills they bring to their role. It is within diversity that an agreement on the common good can be made, not through the editing out of difference.

Students who arrive at an HEI will have received different levels of equipping and preparation for engaging in inter faith dialogue or debate, and may in fact be uncertain of their own beliefs let alone the beliefs of others. Chaplaincies must maintain their long-standing commitment to create spaces where people can mature in their own beliefs and be engaged by people who are different from themselves.

B6.3 What challenges do students from faith communities face?

Issues, among others, that were considered:

- What causes students of faith to be misperceived and misrepresented?
- Do Iraq and the 'War on Terror' affect student needs?
- What difference does having faith activities on campus make?
- What could improve religious students' experience of HE?

Findings

Students' previous experience of community cohesion, in particular between the faith communities, may vary significantly from what they discover in an HE setting. A lack of experience in dialogue, encounter and friendship may mean that individuals are reluctant to engage in inter religious conversation once they find themselves in an HEI setting. Structured opportunities for dialogue can be very beneficial as a route for collaborative modes of learning about world religions in a way that relates to a subject discipline. Having physical chaplaincy spaces within which structured dialogue can occur was considered by several practitioners to be highly advantageous.

Recommendations

Making provisions at the HEI so that students have the opportunity to express their own identity is something that should be planned for, and where it happens it demonstrates an HEI's commitment to community cohesion in a relevant and specific way. Equipping each new set of arriving students with a sense of security in their own identity is a helpful first step to allow their personal growth through opportunities for self-expression, self-development and dialogue. Misperceptions of religious identity are met well through the design of appropriate contexts for encounter and dialogue. These may be physical contexts, or within the student learning and experience opportunities, and also via volunteering programmes.

For further consideration
There can be a marked difference between the way a student understands their own belonging within the community and faith community prior to coming to their HEI and the way such a student understands it during their time at the institution. There is a reasonable possibility that the institution itself could be perceived to be more or less hospitable towards a person from a faith community. This perception may significantly affect student retention, community cohesion and recruitment. Measuring such a transition may be helpful in more accurately anticipating challenges facing students from religious backgrounds, to ensure there is no loss of personal confidence through becoming a member of the HEI.

B6.4 What might a spiritual care Utopia look like?

Issues, among others, that were considered:

- Are religions an opportunity for, or a threat to, social cohesion?
- How can religion and belief issues be met in a secular context?
- Might faith communities transform models of chaplaincy?

Findings
Despite varying views on what a good chaplaincy might look like, eight undergirding principles were recommended for chaplaincies to reach their full potential. They are: spirituality, enquiry, respect, pastoral care, engagement, advocacy, education, and formation. Together these eight principles will result in chaplaincies that create transformative places of life-long learning where students and staff can develop their own inter religious understanding. Some chaplaincies are, at times, wrongly understood by other departments as offering only pastoral care. This misunderstanding may be made by students and staff who

access the service, or by a range of other services and mangers within the institution. Chaplaincies have the ability to help an HEI recognise the learning opportunities that come from a specialist service.

Recommendations

When these processes are developed by a chaplaincy an HEI's confidence is strengthened to engage with issues of religion and belief, by developing a fuller liaison between practitioners who can enable a community of learners.

A chaplaincy should be understood as providing a pastoral and spiritual service as well as being a service that facilitates enquiry, fosters respect, encourages engagement, provides advocacy, develops educational opportunities and empowers learners in their self-formation. Although such a self-definition of chaplaincy may not require a change of nomenclature or departmental position it could require a major change in attitude, within the chaplaincy itself and across the institution.

For further consideration

Chaplaincies can succeed when they are better understood as services that

- o   liaise and interconnect effectively with other services that share the objective to help meet the pastoral, spiritual and academic aspirations of the institution's students and staff
- o   are places where critical thinking and learning occur. Ensuring that there are opportunities to develop teaching and learning, as part of a holistic service, will benefit both the service and the wider institution.

Ensuring that these purposes are better understood by other departments, faith societies and faith communities will help chaplaincies to fulfil their potential.

B7 Student faith societies and HE chaplaincies

B7.1 How can HE chaplaincies help support student faith societies?

Issues, among others, that were considered:

- How are student faith societies and chaplaincies working together?
- What might the 'rights and responsibilities' of a faith society include?
- How can chaplaincies and religious societies work together to promote social cohesion and foster good relations on campus?
- How do chaplaincies engage with societies for New Religious Movements?

Findings
Continuity year on year for student-led societies is a challenge that can be helped by national organisations and local chaplaincies. Chaplaincy staff are well placed to offer professional advice and support. Some religious students and staff will regard their chaplaincy's engagement in inter religious dialogue as going beyond parameters they deem appropriate. Although chaplaincies may be confident about their ability to provide advice and guidance, some with other religious and belief positions may think that the chaplaincy is not the place that will be able to provide them with appropriate support. Some, though, who are unclear about the nature of the faith communities they encounter in the HEI may well turn to the chaplaincy for support and guidance.

Recommendations
Chaplaincies are ideally placed to be a route for providing support for faith societies. Chaplaincies should complement the work of national supporting bodies and the local faith communities. Chaplaincies are particularly well placed to provide context-specific advice, help with networking, and be a relatively independent point of reference for both the Students' Union and the societies. Effective chaplaincies can foster deeper understanding within a particular HEI between people at the institution who have diverse religions and beliefs. Chaplaincies should use their religious expertise to engage rather than ignore those from New Religious Movements.

Where societies are not directly affiliated to the Students' Union, there is scope to be connected to a chaplaincy instead. Chaplaincies can also help with the very significant work of dialogue between different religious groups and encourage movement away from insularity to interest in the other as a way of understanding society and the self more fully, thus promoting social cohesion.

For further consideration
Being a member of an HEI with a varied mix of religions and beliefs creates an opportunity for inter religious understanding and dialogue, though this is often missed due to the natural bonding that occurs between like-minded people. Others may be unintentionally or intentionally excluded from dialogue because they adhere to beliefs or religious practice that are little understood or sit outside the world faiths others have most often encountered. Creating deeper learning experiences requires both strategic thinking and staff who are experienced not only in dialogue, but also in facilitating others to develop confidence in new encounters.

B7.2 Where are student faith societies valued and included in HE?

Issues, among others, that were considered:

- What are the advantages and disadvantages of a student religious society being affiliated to: chaplaincy, Students' Union/Guild, external groups?
- How else do HEIs demonstrate that they value student faith societies?
- Do students of different gender, sexuality, nationality and disability find themselves excluded from societies they would want to participate in?
- Are New Religious Movements valued differently from world religions in HE?

Findings
HEIs and Students' Unions were deemed, by some of the practitioners involved in the dialogue, to have a default mode of being explicit in promoting student societies that excelled in sporting achievement and silent when it came to the religious groups. An example offered counter to this was of an HEI's Access Team enlisting the assistance of a faith society to help with a group visit of Malaysians to the HEI who were Muslim. Practitioners agreed that when diverse faith societies work together it is more likely that they will be appreciated and promoted by the Students' Union and across the HEI.

Affiliation of societies to external bodies may cause certain internal tensions between the chaplaincy and a faith society. These tend to occur where chaplaincy staff have a different theology, ethic or philosophy of practice from that of the external body a society affiliates to. One positive benefit of affiliation to an external body is that societies from different HEIs agree a common set of principles that can create cohesion across a national network.

Recommendations

There is a marketing value that can be attached to an HEI that has a thriving set of religious societies. Chaplaincies may be useful in helping Students' Union, Guild and HEI managers to gain confidence in speaking about the successes of the institution's religious societies. There will be a delicate balance to keep when celebrating the successes of one society, so that this is not experienced by others as institutional bias towards one religion or group. This is particularly important for those from very small religious minorities, for examples Jains and Zoroastrians, so that their identity is also valued and included even if there are not sufficient numbers to sustain a formal society. One way of doing this can be by inviting visitors from small faith communities for special events, seminars or on the occasion of a festival.

It is important that HEIs, chaplaincies, faith communities, Students' Unions and student faith societies themselves do not assume that students' religious needs are being met entirely through any one particular student society, especially where equality issues (including gender, sexuality, disability and ethnicity) are concerned.

For further consideration

Although equality issues were raised as a matter for consideration with practitioners, little was said, except to identify this as a significant issue; further guidance on how to address these substantial matters is pressing. HEIs would benefit from collating optionally provided information from students on religion and belief, and again guidance on how this can be done appropriately is needed, and is raised in 'Conclusions and Next Steps'. For further discussion of equal access to religious provision see Sections B1.2, B2.2 and B4.1.

B7.3 Religion and Belief as an aspect of student experience

Issues, among others, that were considered:

- Student faith societies and chaplaincies foster personal and moral development in members; how else can HEIs support holistic learning?

- What role can religious societies have in encouraging an inclusive curriculum?
- Improved provision for religious students costs. What are the priorities?

Findings
Many examples were shared of how societies and chaplaincies do foster personal and moral development. Examples mentioned by practitioners included special events, educational visits to places of worship, inter religious activities and the inclusion of religion and belief within existing diversity programmes. The question how else student experience can support learning in this area was most specifically addressed by the National Union of Students strategy which has set five priorities that emphasise:

o   training faith societies' leaders
o   organizing a faiths symposium
o   beginning a research project on religious students' involvement in Student Union life
o   developing student volunteering to include cross-community and cross-religious opportunities
o   campaigning for appropriate support for the religious and belief needs of students using a context-specific approach.

Recommendations
The strategic thinking of the NUS demonstrates the ability to respond with confidence to the diverse profile of UK students in a way that relates to members' concerns and interests; interested groups and organisations should support them in their commitments and request feedback on progress made. HEIs and Students' Unions will benefit from paying close attention to the NUS proposals, participating where appropriate and modelling their local practice according to similar principles. Priority-setting like this is most effectively done as a result of collaborative thinking with the people whose needs are to be met, and therefore the NUS should seek to continue to collaborate with national chaplaincy advisors, the Inter Faith Network and national coordinating groups for faith societies.

For further consideration
The same principles that the NUS has adopted can also be applied to curriculum and service development. All members of an HEI are able to consider questions of diversity in their planning, and it is feasible for

faith communities to be invited to offer their perspectives on making the learning experience more inclusive and accessible. One specific example is that of curriculum development. The principle of academic freedom must also be tested to ensure that curriculum developments do not, unnecessarily, marginalise the religions and beliefs of learners.

B7.4 The values of inter-society and inter faith collaboration?

Issues, among others, that were considered:

- Are there some issues that most faith societies have in common?
- How can common religious concerns be articulated and by whom?
- How different is an inter faith forum from a multi faith society?
- What part can chaplaincies play in facilitating collaboration?

Findings

There are relatively few inter religious societies (see Section A: A13) and even where there is connectivity between societies representing different religions, sustained dialogue is hard to maintain. Chaplains both model good practice and energise groups and individuals to cross boundaries and encounter difference. The chaplain's role is particularly important since the predominant culture is agnostic and secular within public life and the HE setting, so the chaplain is likely to have an exceptional familiarity and confidence about religion and belief issues and can serve as a champion and catalyst for dialogue.

Recommendations

Societies that have as one of their purposes developing their members' inter religious understanding are particularly valuable in developing a cohesive HEI environment. Such societies could easily be assumed by others to be responsible for being campaigning bodies on religion and belief needs in an HEI. This would be both unrealistic and unfair since student societies will, typically, be fully taken up with building relationships both internally as well as within and beyond the institution, and also with planning events, fund-raising and ensuring continuity. Although chaplaincy staff cannot be a neutral presence they should be (and often are) informed both in relation to the HEI and on matters of inter religious co-operation and understanding. Chaplains are usually well placed to collaborate with faith societies in organizing faith celebrations and other events, for example 'faith weeks', that are informative and participatory. Additionally, it is vital that HEIs themselves do ensure dialogue, celebration and representation, and that wherever possible collaboration between religions is encouraged, fostered and supported.

For further consideration
The inter faith collaboration that is already happening in HEIs is to be celebrated. Those who are both supporting and leading the way on this are to be applauded: faith societies, chaplaincies, national bodies, Students' Unions, management groups, Equality and Diversity officers, Student Services' heads and faith communities themselves. The HEIs that want to create a holistic learning experience for their students and staff in and out of the classroom will benefit from supporting and growing such collaborations. HEIs will also benefit from considering how dialogue can occur where equalities issues intersect, for example, between cultural, racial and religious issues. The results will be deepened understanding between people with different perspectives, within and beyond the institution, and this can serve as a primary tool for community cohesion by creating new learning, social and cultural environments in higher education.

C. Practice Narratives

Explanatory note: The narratives were collaboratively written between practitioners and the project officer. The findings, recommendations and suggestions for further consideration were written by the project officer alone.

C1 A collegiate university increases its chaplaincy space

Type of activity	*Activity organiser(s)*
A chaplaincy is working, in conjunction with HEI authorities, to make space available to help meet the various needs of the many faiths.	The Chaplain to HEI staff, Central University Council, support from the Vice-Chancellor and the HEI's Estate Management Board.
Involvement	*Context*
The new centre is used by the Chaplaincy, academic departments, Counselling service, faith societies and groups (including a student and staff faith forum), welfare and caring groups and individual student and staff members.	A chaplaincy in a collegiate HEI secured the use of a building that would soon be redundant on a new expansion site to provide community meeting rooms and specific prayer spaces for students and staff of all world faiths. The Multi-Faith Chaplaincy Centre has become a centrally important location in the life of the site.

Description: The renovated building is on a site that, unlike the colleges, has no chapel. It was refurbished to meet the needs of the identified user groups. This includes a kitchen, coffee lounge, meeting room, chaplain's office, 'multi-faith' prayer room, bathroom and toilet—all downstairs. Upstairs there is an Islamic prayer room and a Christian prayer room (these two Faith groups are the main user groups). Historically, spiritual and pastoral care has fallen outside of the remit of central University structures and this has provided the first real sense of a central University provision in this area, taking into account the changing nature of the University and the fact that sizeable numbers of staff (post-doctoral students in particular) are no longer necessarily members of colleges as had almost always previously been the case.

Strengths
This is the first chaplaincy space owned by the HEI rather than by one of the colleges of the HEI, and is set aside to meet the needs of students and staff of all world faiths. This sends out a very strong message to all that equality of provision is now a priority within the HEI as a whole. It also shows that the HEI is beginning to take responsibility for provision in an area it has traditionally believed is the remit of colleges.
Weaknesses
In reality there is barely any official provision for faiths except for Anglican Christians. This new building emphasises existing deficiencies in this area. However this issue is worth exposing because it has encouraged existing support structures and caring agencies to examine and reconsider what provision there is, within the central structures of the HEI and within the college system.
Opportunities
The success of a 'real and living' chaplaincy space has led to architectural provision being made by planners for future sites. It has been extremely helpful in encouraging multi-faith activity and inter faith dialogue. The initiative may provide a model that can influence collegiate approaches to chaplaincy provision.
Threats
The current space is relatively small and will soon be unable to meet the demand being made upon it.

Next Steps: The Chaplaincy is now seeking to move to bigger premises, with a specific budget commitment from the central University to help with the ongoing provision of facilities and so on. This pioneering work has led to increased activities between the many Faith Societies and the University. These groups and societies are now speaking positively about their future within the life and work of the University.

Findings
There is a significant number of HEIs with provision in terms of space and human resource for a single faith group (and this is most commonly Anglican Christians). Although there is a tradition of an inclusive approach in many Anglican chapels and chaplaincies, it is important for those with much in the way of resource to consider how to meet the religious and belief needs of those less well served in the existing structures of an HEI. It is likely, as is the case in this example, that new

assistance comes from other areas of an HEI to support an agenda for providing inter religious hospitality.

Recommendations

When considering adjustments to existing chaplaincy provision of space, it is important to note the inclusivity of the spaces that are already available. Buildings that are dedicated for Christian worship cannot easily serve as inter religious centres. Developing new spaces requires careful consultation with student faith groups, existing chaplaincies, and the Facilities officers at the HEI. Beginning with a trial or temporary centre may make short-term savings but is far more costly in terms of human resource implications for the chaplains who are attempting to manage these changes in provision.

For further consideration

An HEI with a Christian foundation may need to address its religion and belief provision differently from other HEIs. Such an HEI may start from a position of being very well resourced in provision for the religion that established the foundation. However, the same issues are to be faced — namely, considering how much of the existing religious and belief provision is to be maintained and enhanced and how much new provision is needed now and in the future. Committing one or more chaplains to developing a new centre that is a temporary facility could commit excessive staff time over a five to ten year period.

C2 Dialogue events between different faiths

Type of activity	Activity organiser(s)
Informal small group meetings	Chaplaincy and deputy director of Student Services

Involvement	Context
Students, staff, chaplaincy, and Student Services	A chaplaincy already providing key contacts for faiths, and liaising with student faith societies, was seeking, with Student Services to develop further dialogue between religious students and staff.

Description: One example of an event was a dialogue where a Jewish and Muslim speaker shared with one another on topics such as their religion, customs and practice. Those who attended also had opportunity to ask questions and comment.

Strengths

This activity allowed dialogue between the faiths to develop, and points of similarity and understanding to be expressed within a secure environment. It was part of ongoing process to ensure that, in addition to provision for different groups, understanding between them was enhanced. At the same time, collaboration between the chaplaincy and Student Services in order to develop inter religious understanding was promoted.

Weaknesses

The title of the event and the accompanying publicity were deliberately low-key and so attracted a smaller audience than one that would have been more contentious. This avoided creating unnecessary conflict. Those with strongly conflicting perspectives would not have been attracted to such a meeting, and may have been harder to engage with constructively in dialogue.

Opportunities

This event has allowed members of the institution to imagine further dialogue events in the future.

Threats

Such conversations work well with those already committed to inter religious understanding, but people of goodwill are required to sustain them.

Next Steps: It is anticipated that the dialogue events will continue, and that further members of the HEI will have the opportunity to engage with them.

Findings

Small group dialogue events are very likely to build deeper relationships more rapidly between interested parties than high profile one-off events where contrasting views are debated. Creation of events requires the careful identification of people who are at a stage in their own religious, spiritual, intellectual and personal journey at which they are comfortable with participating in and facilitating such conversation. Where such conversations are begun the benefit to all those involved can be very high.

Recommendations

It is a very worthwhile, and yet different, task to find people of different faiths who are willing to be conversation partners in a public setting. This requires skillful discernment from those working in chaplaincy or in another role in an HEI, and also depends on trust having been built up over time. This level of dialogue is well worth aspiring to, and is less likely to lead to adverse or confused publicity than large-scale inter religious events or occasions.

For further consideration

If an HEI is not succeeding in facilitating inter religious dialogue among colleagues and students, then the institution and its members will benefit from considering what more it could do to ensure that it is a place of mutual respect, enquiry and collaboration in the sphere of religious life and practice.

C3 An act of worship for One World Week

Type of activity	*Activity organiser(s)*
A Christian act of worship that served also as an inclusive inter faith event.	Local 'Churches Together', a student society looking at faith, arts, culture and education, local Hindu representatives, and a College chaplain.
Involvement	*Context*
Members of the College and University, the inter religious student faith society, attendees from local churches and faith communities, local residents.	The College chaplaincy had historically provided for Christian students and staff of the institution. The engagement in One World Week opened up an opportunity to address issues of concern from people of a variety of political, cultural and religious perspectives.

Description: The organised activity was a Christian service of worship, but one that attempted to be inclusive. A Jewish student read from the Hebrew Scriptures, and an International Student talked about 'his world' in Sri Lanka.

Strengths

This was significant both for being collaborative between the local community and university and also for engaging with people from different faith groups.

Weaknesses

It was difficult to find representation from every faith. Responsibility for managing the event fell mainly to the chaplain, which meant there was less practical collaboration than was hoped for.

Opportunities

This is likely to lead to further events in the future coordinated in a way that will encourage further collaboration between different groups in the planning and running of the event.

Threats

One particular student faith society at the College which expressed anxieties about inter religious activities was unhappy at the change in approach by the chaplain. This is being addressed through sustained dialogue with them. Also, because the event was dependent on the work of the chaplain, expectations about future activities will need to change to prevent the responsibility all falling to one person.

Next Steps: It is hoped this model can be both sustained and developed further

Findings
The number of inter religious student societies is increasing but is still small compared with single faith societies. Where such groups are succeeding, the chaplaincy is typically a key contributor. This particular event drew together effectively the energies of the student society, religious representatives from the local community and an existing church in the area. Community collaboration such as this is commendable.

Recommendations
When a variety of groups work together at the outset of a new project, it is likely that lines of responsibility will tend to be quite fluid. This is particularly so when church and faith groups, student societies, and chaplaincies are involved. Therefore, it is important if good communication is to be sustained that a steering group or something similar is established as early as possible. This will help ensure that the initial cohesion can serve as the starting point for good ongoing collaboration.

For further consideration
Collaborative partnership may require empowerment by those who already have some ability to facilitate smaller or less established groups. An HEI can, through sponsorship, make the difference to whether such events are sustained or not.

C4 Developing a new chaplaincy centre

Type of activity	Activity organiser(s)
Liaison by the lead chaplain with the HEI's Senior Management Team (SMT), facilities directorate as well as with chaplaincy team members and the student faith societies to develop a new chaplaincy centre.	Lead Chaplain and the Facilities Directorate.

Involvement	Context
The Chaplain, SMT, Facilities directorate, chaplaincy team members, Student Services, and student faith societies.	A Chaplaincy already providing advisors for seven faiths, and a prayer room for all faiths including Islamic prayer facilities, is planning the development of a more appropriate and accessible centre including improved prayer spaces.

Description: The existing prayer space was inadequate, especially for Muslim prayer, and spaces of varying quality were dispersed around the HEI. Any development work was determined to demonstrate an equality of provision for all and the meeting of specific and distinctive needs at the same time.

Strengths
Starting with a new space gave the opportunity for a more coordinated approach to provision and brought the prayer rooms for Muslims more directly under the umbrella of Student Services and the chaplaincy. This will lead to a clearer and more distinctive service provision and encourage further inter religious understanding by drawing together people from a variety of backgrounds to share the same space.

Weaknesses
The new space (which is being developed as a 'multi-faith' chaplaincy centre) overlays the space of what were the existing Muslim prayer rooms. The space previously offered was in a prominent location and yet limited. What has been the largest

prayer room will, in the new development, also need to function as a meeting room so that no particular faith has ownership of it. It is likely that conflicting types of use of this space will create new tensions.

Opportunities

This development has allowed for a much closer liaison between the chaplaincy and the Islamic society in particular because of the transition from separate facilities to a large shared space.

Threats

Encouraging a range of faith groups to use the same space, and managing the transition between events and between different student societies, are likely to be time consuming for the lead chaplain. In addition, good relations cannot be guaranteed, only worked towards, and this physical model is dependent on good relations for effective use of a multi-use religious facility.

Next Steps: It will be important to continue to consult with those using the centre both prior to and after the completion of the new facility. Careful monitoring of the success of the project, and the consideration of similar provision across the HEI's multiple societies, will become a new priority.

Findings
HEIs that already have some prayer facilities and want to improve their provision are commonly faced with the challenge of replacing existing spaces with something that is more multi-purpose and suitable for use by all faiths — especially when existing space is not integral to the HEI's foundation. A motivation for change may come in part from the desire by the HEI to convert spaces dedicated for use by one faith group into something that is more suitable for use by many different religious groups so that there is less inequality of provision.

Recommendations
HEIs that attempt to make more equal provision by diminishing what is already in place for specific faith groups must be very cautious. Such action will be very challenging to faith community members whose space is diminished and who may feel aggrieved as a result. Furthermore, chaplaincy staff and others who manage the space will face numerous challenges in overseeing such a transition. There is a high risk of negative consequences in terms of the amount of time chaplaincy staff may have to spend in mediating the HEIs decision and then

managing the use of multi-purpose space(s). There is also a possibility that such spaces may not succeed in operating effectively where a physical space is set aside in the conviction that it is possible to design "one size that fits all". Another risk is that although one space may in principle be able to accommodate everyone, it is possible that one group will make much more use of the space than others. Consequently, perceived ownership may begin to reside with those who use it most — which could defeat the original purpose of the change.

For further consideration
A close study of the relevant legislation and a subsequent legal interpretation at local level, combined with an assessment of all risks involved in acting or not acting, must be undertaken prior to adjustments or developments of chaplaincy centres and other such facilities. Visits should be made to existing spaces in other HEIs and frank questions asked about the success of schemes that have been completed in recent years. An HEI must endeavour to develop spaces that are both symbolic and practical.

C5 Establishing a Religious Equality and Diversity Group

Type of activity	*Activity organiser(s)*
A group was convened by the University Equality and Diversity Advisor and chaired by the Chaplain. Several aims included promoting a better understanding of faith and belief issues in the University and supporting the implementation of the University's faith and belief policy.	University Chaplain, Equality and Diversity officer and group members of diverse faith backgrounds across the University.
Involvement	*Context*
All staff through group emails, student group emails and Student Union emailing, diversity group members, local faith communities and worship centres.	A chaplain who became more integral to HEI life by becoming part of Student Services and networking with the Equality and Diversity Advisor became the chair of a new group.

Description: The group was established to address religious equality and diversity issues in the institution. Outcomes of the group's meetings have included advertised trips to local places of worship and occasional email announcements to staff about selected religious festivals.

Strengths
A joint approach by interested parties in the HEI allows the chaplain to be influential but ensures that the strategic development of provision for all faiths does not depend on the chaplaincy alone. The Equality and Diversity officer who has responsibility for all issues of access in this institution is supported in their role by the chaplain, and vice versa. The regular emails sent to students and staff and the visits to places of worship help raise the place of faith/belief within the HEI. Previously, the only formally endorsed religious activity of the institution was the carol service. Now, a range of events and festivals is organised by the institution. This shows respect for the diverse backgrounds, religions and beliefs of those who are members of the HEI.

Weaknesses

This is a management-centred approach to provision for faiths and is largely staff-led. Student liaison has not, as yet, been a key feature of this work. However, this is being addressed by events that are organised for students, which lead to informal liaison that in turn encourages creative conversations about future activities. The group depends on the goodwill and time of volunteers. Attendance at meetings is often poor — that may also be due to geographical distances involved in making journeys — and staff having to come from different college locations. Also, while a shared action plan/notes are agreed at meetings, it is usually the responsibility of one or two members (usually the Chaplain and the Diversity Advisor) to get things done.

Opportunities

The work of this group has already resulted in the raising of the profile of 'faith and belief' mainly through the occasional emails sent out to all staff around the dates of major religious festivals. A study visit to a place of worship for staff and students of the HEI went well — the plan is to do something similar once each term. The group has also given members some sense of identity (the group was set up alongside others — Disability, Sexual Orientation, Black Minority Ethnic — under the umbrella of the Equal Opportunities Forum) and also a voice within a secular educational setting that is at best perplexed by its members of faith/belief. It has also given the Chaplain a greater degree of access to staff of faith/belief through the label of 'diversity' than that of 'Chaplain' — which is still widely perceived as exclusively Christian/Church of England. It has raised the profile of the Chaplain and linked chaplaincy explicitly to the diversity agenda.

Threats

The new group was established first, and so the inter faith ethic is being constructed in situ. As yet no points of major disagreement have occurred in the group. If in the future there were to be a major conflict of views, the group might not function so well. Nothing has yet been put in place to guard against this. At one point, the group appeared to begin to focus its energies solely on prayer rooms. This was partly because of a lack of provision and partly because of the interests of group members. The members of the group understand, however, the broader and more creative opportunities they have for effecting long-term change — not just for people of faith and belief, but within the culture of the University.

Next Steps: These are uncertain at this stage: the group will have spent a term 'treading water' due to the absence of the Diversity Advisor. One of the things to do on an annual basis is to advertise the group's existence to staff and students and to implement a plan to recruit new members.

Findings

There is merit in an HEI wanting to consider various equality issues together. When planning to meet religion and belief needs, it is important that any actions cohere with provision for the intersecting demands of disability, gender, ethnicity, sexuality and social inclusion responsibilities. Collaboration between chaplaincy and Equality and Diversity staff is an effective way for an HEI to engage with this challenge, in order to connect these different strands.

Recommendations

Where an HEI establishes a formal structure aiming to strengthen its provision for religious and belief needs, appropriate and sustained representation from a variety of religious backgrounds and from the student and staff community is important.

For further consideration

Sustaining such a group relies in part on the efforts of the salaried Equality and Diversity and chaplaincy staff. Other staff and student members of an HEI are required to volunteer their time, so success depends on their enthusiasm and availability. Chaplaincy involvement in such a group can only be beneficial, but the committee is unlikely to succeed without community co-operation. In order to develop more substantial provision for religious and belief needs, it is worth considering such work in conjunction with efforts to recruit community volunteers.

C6 Development of a chaplaincy centre including prayer facilities

Type of activity	Activity organiser(s)
Liaison between the chaplaincy team, Student Services, Estates and student groups.	University Chaplain, Estates, Student Services.

Involvement	Context
The Chaplaincy, Muslim and Christian chaplains, the Estates director.	A chaplaincy already providing prayer space for faiths, and in friendly contact with student faith societies, was seeking to develop a new centre, which would allow greater access and an improved and more equal provision of prayer facilities.

Description: The existing spaces for prayer and chaplaincy staff were spread out and not as accessible as they might have been. New build freed up existing space which Student Services allocated to become a new chaplaincy centre.

Strengths

Such a development allows closer collaboration between the religious student societies who want to use prayer spaces and the chaplaincy. People of different faiths are encouraged to liaise and deepen their understanding of one another. Where in the past there was a prospect of intra-faith conflicts, the new arrangement provides a springboard for new ways of co-operating, and allows some governance of student activity.

Weaknesses

Some religious societies are cautious about coming under the authority of the chaplaincy and would prefer greater autonomy.

Opportunities

Once opened, the new centre will allow inter religious co-operation to flourish through improved networking.

Threats
Muslim students are likely to have the largest presence in the centre due to the prayer facilities being sited there. Other faith groups may begin to feel marginalised in comparison. Other groups are being encouraged to have their meetings, informal social occasions and prayer events at the centre in order to address this.

Next Steps
This project is work in progress.

Findings
The threat to the success of such a centre is great. To combine all the physical space provided for religious and belief needs at an HEI into one place may be a laudable aspiration but may result in one faith group becoming the dominant user. Others may feel marginalised within a shared space, thus demolishing the ethic that had motivated the construction of an environment that could serve all needs.

Recommendations
Provision for different religious groups cannot principally be expressed through a physical space, since religions require varying amounts of space at different levels of frequency. Space provision is only one of several priorities in relation to religious needs at an HEI. There is a danger that making physical spaces needs the first or only priority may, in fact, engender further inequality.

For further consideration
Having a centre run by the chaplaincy for student religious activity has benefits, but may also have the effect of sending underground any religious groups that do not feel comfortable co-operating with the chaplaincy. A more fluid approach to facilitating student religious activity is usually going to be appropriate in an HEI.

C7 Developing a team of chaplaincy faith advisors

Type of activity	Activity organiser(s)
Building a team and advertising the provision	University Chaplains

Involvement	Context
The chaplaincy staff including existing faith advisors	Three denominational chaplaincies have been serving a post '92 university. Two Muslim advisors joined the team in the 90s. Collaboration with Student Services had previously been minimal.

Description: The chaplaincy's faith advisor team was extended by the involvement of existing contacts from the Hindu and Sikh communities known to the Anglican chaplain. Then the photographs of the four Christian, two Muslim, one Hindu and one Sikh team members were printed up on posters and postcards and distributed throughout the university. The university paid for the publicity and concurrently provided a temporary space for the chaplains.

Strengths

The HEI has moved from keeping the chaplaincies outside the university site to supporting and promoting their work and choosing to include them in the new Student Services centre. The Director of Student Experience is also now meeting with the team regularly to brief them. This new development has encouraged better liaison.

Weaknesses

Previously the denominational chaplaincies struggled for recognition by the university. Now they are finding that the new attention and new expectations lead to misunderstandings, which have to be clarified. The process will be positive one in the long term but requires a cautious approach at the outset. Misguided thinking from the institution about what chaplaincy can and cannot provide must be addressed.

Opportunities

The creation of a team has already led to the chaplaincy not only being consulted about the prayer spaces which had previously been managed and at times controlled by student societies, but also being given authority over them. Although granting students autonomy over space might have its benefits, the disadvantage was that there was evidence of an inequality of provision for one faith community compared to others. The institution's uncertainty of how to intervene has changed to a confident dependency on the advice of the faith advisors and chaplains to ensure a better approach in the future.

Threats

Student groups will have to adjust to a new arrangement where the chaplaincy will manage faith issues from within the Student Services team. In the past it was the Students' Union that had the primary responsibility for this. Ultimately, the university will be seen to be providing a better level of service to religious students. In the short term, students may regard themselves as losing existing rights.

Next Steps: The transition into the new physical location is now being followed by a period of adjustment and agenda-setting.

Findings

There may be various historical reasons for a chaplaincy team consisting of some faith representatives and not others. For HEIs and chaplaincies that aspire to develop a chaplaincy that includes specialist staff or advisors, and to achieve this in a measured and equivalent way, the process can be time consuming and challenging. It is likely to happen slowly, and may also result in some readjustments for existing team members.

Recommendations

An ideal that many HEI chaplaincies have missed is establishing a collaborative inter religious team where equivalent levels of support are offered and wide representation is drawn upon from the outset. For those growing new teams the benefits of taking a holistic approach cannot be exaggerated.

For further consideration

At some HEI student faith societies have had a history of taking the lead on religious issues. The transition of responsibility to members of staff teams, who become the new negotiators and assessors, requires careful management.

C8 Establishing a multi-faith society

Type of activity	*Activity organiser(s)*
The inter faith society exists to promote friendships among students belonging to various faiths. The meetings of the inter faith society include:	The events and meetings of the society are organised entirely by a committee of students. The chaplaincy is committed to supporting the work of the society in whatever way the students wish. The chaplaincy will not interfere in the running or strategic direction of the society.

1. Regular scripture study sessions, where scriptures from various faiths on a given topic, for example 'peace', are read and discussed

2. Visits to different places of worship, for example, a Gudwara, Hindu temple, Baha'i centre, and synagogue. Visits often include a tour, an introduction to the faith and its rituals and a meal.

3. Discussions on a given theme, for example 'food'. Since there is a danger of the discussions becoming a source of discord, the themes remain topics relating to faith (such as God and rules to be followed) and less to overt politics.

4. Socials, including icebreaker games and movie nights, with a film shown that promotes inter religious or inter cultural harmony.

5. An exhibition of some aspects of different faiths. A workshop took place that included Hindu meditation, a Baha'i tranquility zone and Buddhist martial art.

6. The society contributes to inter faith meetings, over food, which is organised by the chaplaincy's Multi-faith reference group (for example on the theme of 'Faith and the Environment').

Involvement	Context
Students, the chaplaincy (including the Multi-faith Reference Group), local places of worship and local faith communities.	A chaplaincy already providing prayer space for all the world religions, and in friendly contact with student faith societies, was seeking to develop further dialogue between religious students. This was out of concern for the quality of the student experience at the HEIs the chaplaincy relates to. This is understood by the chaplaincy to be part of its ministry of hospitality and care to students and staff.

Description: During the summer of 2006 a group of students from different faith traditions took the creative step of establishing a student inter faith society. A chaplain and the International Chaplain offered support. This led the chaplaincy's Multi-faith reference group and the society meeting together for a meal. The reference group now includes representation from the inter faith society. A range of visits to different places of worship, inter faith discussions and an inter faith meal were organised for the first term's programme.

Strengths

Support from the chaplaincy ensures the group can be sustained in terms of provision of space, expenses and staff time. The collaborative approach between students and chaplaincy staff (and the Multi-faith Reference Group) ensures an improved quality of dialogue.

Weaknesses

Support for the society depends on the hard work of the chaplaincy, and during the first year the critical mass of interested parties may fall off as the pressure of the academic year increases.

Opportunities

Existing societies for faith groups may be committed to dialogue and inter religious understanding, but they appreciate a new society, which they can go to rather than having to organise to meet with people of different faiths. This new group is also encouraging societies to liaise directly with one another, too.

Threats

Some religious students might be opposed to a group that is called 'inter faith'. There might even be debate over what the nature of such a student society might be. It is realistic to anticipate that some students may suggest an alternative inter faith or multi-faith society independent from the current process. This would have to be addressed by giving time to educating people about the society in addition to the society's objective of allowing members to educate themselves about one another.

Next Steps: The society hopes to maintain the present level of activity and to have a structure where the continuity of the society is ensured by the different student faith societies. The hope is to get registered as a Students' Union society. The intention is to support faith society events such as Islamic Awareness week. The chaplaincy's Multi-faith Reference Group plans to engage with inter religious issues through a day conference and local faith community engagement and to broaden its representation. This is to help forward the debate about the place and contribution of faith in Higher Education.

Findings

Chaplaincies and student societies can usually cooperate. However, there is always the risk that some students will want to work differently or separately from figures that they perceive to be in authority.

Recommendations

When a new student society or an inter faith forum is founded, it is important to identify to all those wanting to be involved

- o   what the nature of the collaboration is
- o   who has the final say
- o   who has the power to change the way such a group is run.

Chaplaincies can be instrumental in supporting such groups, but too much involvement leads to too much control. The group's autonomy must be preserved, so a careful positioning of engagement by chaplains is very important.

For further consideration
In the past many chaplaincies have supported student faith societies that have represented one religion or a single religious perspective. For a chaplaincy to be able to support a society that has an inter faith outlook, appropriate recruitment of staff and a commitment to inter religious understanding and co-operation is essential.

C9 Building a new Muslim prayer facility with external funding

Type of activity	Activity organiser(s)
Drawing on external funding to build a new Muslim prayer room	HEI's chaplain, Estates department, HEI's Islamic Society, an external funder.

Involvement	Context
The Chaplaincy, Christian and Muslim students and staff, a Muslim adviser, the external funder, and the relevant university managers and committees.	A Chaplaincy was already providing prayer space for all the faiths. The chaplaincy already had a positive liaison with student faith societies, and was asked by the HEI to facilitate a scoping exercise to determine the size and purpose of a prayer facility for Muslim students funded from an external source. The original intention of the HEI and chaplaincy had been to provide a space for a number of faiths, funded by a range of faith partners. In the event the only offer of moneys came from a Muslim source, so the strategy was modified to put in place provision for Muslim students first. It is still hoped that existing and new spaces can also be developed to improve the facilities for students of the other world faiths.

Description: The amount of funding made available enabled the university to remodel some space to provide a prayer room that could be used by more than a hundred men and fifty women. In addition to the prayer room there are also *wudu* facilities for Islamic washing for both genders and a library of Islamic texts.

Strengths

The provision is of an excellent standard. That the facility is dedicated for Muslim prayer has allowed it to become a 'no shoes' area. It has the appropriate carpeting that demarcates the direction of Mecca and allows Muslim students on a green field site beyond close reach of a mosque to complete their prayers and gather together for the Friday prayer all at once.

Weaknesses

Prior to this development, the adjacent Christian chaplaincy centre was made available equally to all faiths. Although the chaplaincy wants to continue to provide for the needs of students of all beliefs and none, the new provision for one faith means there is now an inequality of provision that will need addressing in the future. Also, the management of the prayer room is currently the responsibility of the Christian chaplain. It may be problematic to assign such a level of responsibility for a Muslim space to a chaplain or advisor from a religion other than Islam.

Opportunities

The development has led to a much-improved relationship between the chaplain and the Muslim students of the university, who have liaised with the chaplaincy and sought support and advice. It may also lead to the appointment of a Muslim chaplain to work with the students and help manage the prayer space.

Threats

External funding has produced a positive outcome for one faith group at the HEI. The risk now is of students of different faiths asking the university to ensure they have an equal provision regardless of funding.

Next Steps: Securing further funding for development of other new facilities is an important aspiration that is yet to be fulfilled.

Findings
Excellent facilities can be developed to provide a high standard of religious space at an HEI when

- o a reasonable amount of space can be found
- o the institution's Senior Management Team is committed to the task

- o   the chaplaincy is supportive
- o   an external source of funding is available.

In this instance, a substantial proportion of the sponsorship was external and ownership is internal to the HEI. Three significant shortcomings are:

- o   the aspiration for an inter religious centre was not realised
- o   the quality of provision for one faith exceeds provision for others
- o   a site visit suggested that there is a variety of views about the facility's name, some regarding it as a prayer room, while others understand it to be a mosque.

Recommendations

When an HEI is choosing to develop its provision for the religious and belief needs of students and staff by opening new physical spaces, it needs to be managed as a project to ensure a realistic schedule for developments. It is important to prioritise provision where there is an immediate and pressing need. It is important for an HEI to consider the long term plans for religious and belief needs of students and staff. At all stages of the planning process future requirements need to be anticipated and smaller groups of religious students or those without external sponsors need to be considered.

For further consideration

Many faith groups external to an HEI may be involved in funding the provision of religious spaces or other resources that are used and/or managed by chaplaincies. The most common example of this is the many Christian chaplains, chaplaincies and chapels that are often substantially or at least partially funded by churches. In more than 90% of HEIs the lead chaplain in an HEI is an ordained Christian minister. An increasing number of these lead chaplains are now taking responsibility for managing the various religious spaces on their HEI's campuses.

In order to avoid confusion or conflict later on, the definition of lines of authority and accountability for such spaces (particularly between student faith societies, university managers and chaplaincy managers) is a priority. HEIs should reflect on the benefits of partnership funding, and the transformative influence such new co-operation may have. Collective responsibility for this is advisable as the HEI, the Students' Union, the societies and chaplaincy may all have separate structures of governance and management.

C10 Dialogue event: 'Truth in the Qur'an and Christian Scriptures'

Type of activity	Activity organiser(s)
Public meeting on campus	The Chaplaincy and University Islamic Society

Involvement	Context
The Chaplaincy, Christian and Muslim students and staff, and a Muslim speaker from the local community.	This Chaplaincy was already providing prayer space for all the faiths and has a self-understanding of its operation as 'multi-faith'. The chaplaincy was already in friendly contact with student faith societies and was seeking to develop further dialogue between religious students. It was, therefore, happy to respond positively to the student society's initiative in proposing a debate.

Description: Christian and Muslim speakers were booked and at the start of the autumn term an event was advertised at which truth as presented in the Qur'an and the Christian scriptures would be debated. A range of students and staff attended the event, and contrasting views were expressed by speakers and in questions from the floor. This included some internal debate within the faith groups, and between the speakers and members of the audience. There was chance to discuss points both of convergence and divergence.

Strengths
The meeting allowed dialogue between the faiths to develop, and allowed conflicting viewpoints to be expressed within a secure environment. The event was the outcome of an ongoing process to ensure provision for different groups and the development of understanding between them. At the same time the event helped to promote the Multi-faith chaplaincy's role developing inter religious understanding.

Weaknesses

The title and publicity of the event needed to be provocative enough to attract an audience without being so contentious that either the debate or the impression of the event became distorted. 'The True Word of God: The Qur'an or the Bible' was not considered to be an event that would create unnecessary conflict though it did identify what some points of divergence were. It also led to something of an uneven debate, given that it is difficult to discuss the Bible as isolated from the person of Jesus, yet necessary to discuss the Qur'an as isolated in the same way that Allah is isolated (cf. Tawheed: i.e. the Islamic idea of monotheism).

Opportunities

The event has allowed members of the institution to imagine further dialogue events in the future.

Threats

Media interest in such activities and in the background of speakers can create a risk of misreporting. In this case, the communications department provided support.

---

*Next Steps:*The 'Multi-faith Chaplaincy' at this HEI continues to facilitate an ongoing program of events and dialogues that aims to challenge, inspire and encourage people of all religions and beliefs to engage with religious issues.

Findings
Opportunities for sustained dialogue may well begin with a one-off meeting that becomes a catalyst for further conversations. Beginning with something as high profile as this event has led to some subsequent consideration of the costs and benefits of developing inter religious dialogue with an event that had such a high profile format, and therefore was more at risk of generating unintended negative outcomes.

Recommendations
Occasions such as this can serve as a point of departure in beginning dialogue. It may be counter-productive not to follow up on a one-off event, however, since the opening of a conversation can serve to launch further dialogue. Individuals wanting to participate in sustained dialogue will have to experience challenges to their own world-view that may be unsettling. Futhermore, dialogue partners must themselves negotiate the terms by which a conversation may be sustained.

For further consideration

Dialogue that is focussed on 'scriptural reasoning' has proved to be a successful area for significant development (cf. the 'Cambridge Inter-Faith Programme'), particularly between Christian, Jewish and Muslim conversation partners. An assessment should be made of how different styles of dialogue best suit the intersections between different faith groups (e.g. Abrahamic faiths) in any particular context. Certain styles may work more effectively and new methodologies may need to be developed.

C11 Joint HEI start of academic year service in local Cathedral

Type of activity	Activity organiser(s)
The event is a celebration for students, staff and their friends from two universities in the same city, at the start of the academic year, involving various faith communities.	University chaplaincies, faith community representatives, senior managers at the two HEIs and the Dean and Chapter of the cathedral.
Involvement	*Context*
Officers, students and staff of the two universities, the university 'multi-faith chaplaincies', and other local faith community representatives.	Two chaplaincies with strong connections in a city with two HEIs have developed a joint service that reflects the diversity of both city and members of the HEIs.

Description: This service has developed out of the framework of an Anglican service of evensong for the start of the academic year, and still takes place within that same worship context, within the cathedral's programme of evensongs. Now the service involves representatives from a number of local faith communities, particularly those with named chaplains and student religious societies/groups in the HEIs. The service retains its identity as a Christian act of worship, but it includes within it corporate actions that unite the different faiths.

Strengths
The service proactively engages the local faith communities while maintaining a substantial connection with the majority faith in the locality.

Weaknesses
There are two separate issues that are weaknesses in this approach:

- Some faith adherents from the universities and from local faith communities may be uncomfortable with inter faith gatherings and so not participate.
- Some faith community members may feel unable to take part because it is held in a Cathedral rather than a neutral space.

Opportunities
This event may lead to the development of other inter faith opportunities in associated networks and at the HEIs. It has the potential (and has started) to contribute to greater cohesion within and between the multi-faith chaplaincy teams and to strengthen the links between the HEIs and the local faith communities.

Threats
The success and continuation of the service is dependent on the enthusiasm and the commitment of the current chaplaincy team-leaders and of the Dean and Cathedral Chapter. Its success is also dependent on the willingness of the local faith communities to participate and the support of both HEIs' management groups.

Next Steps: The service is reviewed annually.

Findings
Developing inter religious activities in the context of existing worship, or introducing them into ceremonial occasions, is deeply challenging for the HEI, the participants and the local faith communities. All the same, a small number of HEIs have made considerable efforts in this direction. This narrative describes just one context where an inter religious element has been introduced to worship. In most instances, as here, this has occurred after great consultation and with care, over time. Where inter religious worship takes place, it is also not untypical for it to be introduced into an established act of Christian worship and in a church setting.

Recommendations
HEIs that, by custom and practice, already have religious occasions to mark moments in the university year may benefit from one of three things:

- o   extending the variety of occasions where a religious act takes place
- o   considering how people of different faiths and beliefs are included by different events and occasions throughout the year
- o   exploring when there may be appropriate time to include formal representation from local faith communities at HEI
- o   celebrations and formal occasions.

For further consideration

This research has discovered, within HEIs, many examples of team-working that involves several world religions. However, there is no full agreement about the most appropriate approaches for co-operation, although the guidance from the Inter Faith Network for the UK is an excellent starting point (appendix 5). There are very few examples of inter religious worship being used, within the sector, as an expression of collaboration between different faiths. Attempting to arrange such worship comes from an ideological position that may not be shared by those from local faith communities or from students with a commitment to a world religion or other belief system. A question for those who have already embarked on such initiatives and for those who have not is, whose aspirations are being satisfied by inter religious worship?

C12 Developing chaplaincy support for students of faith

Type of activity	Activity organiser(s)
An HEI chaplaincy provides support to students and staff who are from religious groups and wants to develop this further.	The university chaplaincy.

Involvement	Context
The chaplaincy, the students' faith societies, the university Student Services department and individual staff and students.	This post-1992 university sits close to the edge of a very large conurbation and has a significant proportion of students from Black and Minority Ethnic (BME) groups who are members of organised religions. This proportion is quite different to the demographic of the locality where BME groups make up a smaller proportion of the population.

Description: The Chaplaincy is seeking to develop further support for students and staff through a review process that has identified religion and belief needs and considered best practice in comparable HEIs. Student faith groups have identified the provision of space for religious purposes and contact with local faith communities as more significant than easy access to individual religious advisors. There is a strong local Inter faith Forum in the community, but not all faith groups are adequately represented at this.

The Chaplaincy already has one full-time ecumenical chaplain and one part-time administrator working in paid posts. It anticipates appointing further honorary chaplains or faith advisors in the near future.

Strengths
The current approach responds to student needs in a way that does not impose an existing model of 'chaplaincy' on them. It also emphasises the autonomy of student faith groups. If the proposed new pattern succeeds it will engage local faith communities more fully with the university community.

Weaknesses

The new plans do not guarantee clear representation from local faith communities at the HEI. Nor are there individuals who are responsible for providing advice and points of contact for each faith group.

Opportunities

This HEI chaplaincy has the clear opportunity to strengthen community relations between faith groups in the university and to improve social cohesion between the locality and members of the HEI.

Threats

It may be that if the chaplaincy's development of provision does not succeed, students and staff of faith will become dependent on those already in the institution, which may breed a level of insularity from the local community and weaken the level of provision.

Next Steps: The process of appointing new chaplaincy team members is ongoing.

Findings

A particular challenge presents itself where the diversity of religious and belief perspectives among an HEI's constituency is greater than that in the locality, or localities, in which the institution is situated. Most chaplaincies that provide support for students and staff from different religions and beliefs draw on local community volunteers or on existing members of staff across the HEI. The approach outlined in this narrative seeks to draw on existing networks in the hope that there can be a positive dynamic that can be transformative both of institution and the local community.

Recommendations

An HEI can assist with social cohesion by placing religion and belief matters on the local community's agenda, and engaging with existing structures such as a faiths forum. All HEIs would benefit from supporting such groups. Being dependent on a local inter faith meeting alone to access specialist advice for HEI members may well be unwise, because those involved in such a grouping may not be representative of the strands or traditions of a religion that students or staff at the HEI belong to.

For further consideration

The quality of an HEI's integration with its local context has a significant bearing on how inter religious understanding develops both within and beyond the institution. This is worth assessing and developing. A healthy dynamic can at best lead to demographic change and improved student and staff recruitment. A weak relationship between HEI and locality can at worst lead to tensions between contrasting traditions of one religion and even inter religious tension that compound town and gown differences.

C13 Multi-faith statement of commitment for chaplaincy team

Type of activity	*Activity organiser(s)*
Drawing on the experience of a range of contexts a Multi-faith Statement has been drawn up both for paid and voluntary chaplains. The statement is signed at the start of a chaplain's appointment to signify that they are prepared to work as part of the Multi-faith Team and within the parameters of the Multi-faith Chaplaincy.	The Multi-faith Chaplaincy Committee — the governing body of the Chaplaincy Service — has drawn up The Multi-faith Statement.
Involvement	*Context*
The statement is signed by all chaplains, who commit to work with all members of the University, but not by Faith Contacts, who work only with students and staff from their own faith community.	The statement was developed at the time the chaplaincy became a Multi-faith Chaplaincy. This was to ensure that the Chaplaincy and the University had a commitment from new members of the team that they would work within the parameters set by the Chaplaincy. This was particularly important as the HEI appoints none of the team and the employment/appointment of chaplains is by their faith community and not directly by the Chaplaincy.

Description: Some of the statement draws heavily on Building Good Relations with People of Different Faiths and Beliefs (© the Inter Faith Network for the UK [1993, 2000]), and certain aspects of it do differ from the Inter Faith Network's own text (see Appendix 5 for the full Inter Faith Network's text). The statement speaks of the Chaplains working together as a team, striving for inter religious understanding and co-operation without blurring the differences that exist between the various faith groups represented. It describes how faith is to be respected in the HEI, and how each chaplain will:

- o provide appropriate pastoral care
- o respect difference in viewpoints
- o work within the boundaries of confidentiality
- o cross-refer to another chaplain.

The statement also gives guidance on how one's own faith is to be shared, and on the shared values there are within the team. When it comes to sharing faith there is a stress on having respect for others and speaking of one's commitment in a way that doesn't threaten the other. Commonly shared values of reconciliation, understanding, listening and then responding 'with openness and respect', so as to 'acknowledge genuine differences and build on shared hopes and values' are used to resolve conflict.

Strengths
The statement ensures that the chaplaincy and University have an agreement with the chaplains regarding their role and work methods.

Weaknesses
The statement is generic and covers an individual's commitment in general but not the specific work they will do. This is still agreed informally with the Chaplaincy Team.

Opportunities
This provides a useful model for others to imitate elsewhere. It also allows faith communities that are uncertain of how they are esteemed to make fuller sense of their role within the HEI and chaplaincy and demonstrate their equal footing alongside other faith communities.

Threats
The statement could be open to interpretation and some may be prepared to sign up to some but not all of it. At the moment the statement is non-negotiable but in the future individual statements may need to be considered to reflect different levels of engagement.

Next Steps: It may be appropriate to develop individualised statements that are more specific to the work each member does.

Findings
Statements or working agreements of collaborative intent ensure that chaplaincy staff members understand the parameters within which they must work. When shared beyond the team, these statements

clarify the roles and basis for co-operation both to the HEI and the respective religious groups that the faith representatives come from (who may sponsor the work of one or more individuals).

Recommendations
Wherever there is a staff team working in a chaplaincy where many beliefs, religions and traditions are represented, such statements of commitment can only benefit a collaborative approach. This is important to each member of a chaplaincy team because the sponsorship and funding of each person's role tends to differ, as does each individual's perspective on their vocation and understanding of their role. Having a statement that all sign up to brings some clarity about what equality there is in terms of working, mutual understanding and shared aspirations.

For further consideration
Beyond statements of commitment, there is the possibility of full service level agreements and contracts of employment. It may prove more challenging to ensure contractual parity between volunteers and paid staff, and between those on temporary or permanent or no contract, than with a statement. This is still worth aspiring to both for the chaplaincy, sponsoring religious groups and the HEI.

C14 A Church HEI reflects on its religion and belief provision with the Christian chaplain

Type of activity	Activity organiser(s)
A Church foundation HEI has begun to reflect on its religion and belief provision with the institution's Christian Chaplain.	The HEI's Chief Executive Officer and Chaplain.

Involvement	Context
The HEI's Chief Executive Officer, Chaplain, Director of Student Services, Facilities Manager and International Officer, and a member of the Theology faculty.	This Church foundation institution largely recruits from a mostly white population. Nearly all members of the HEI who are faith adherents are Christian. Due to the HEI's internationalisation and changing demographics within the wider region, staff and student recruitment has begun to change.

Description: Consultations have begun on future provision for religious and belief needs at the HEI. This is due to the HEI's Chief Executive Officer and Chaplain recognizing that there are many benefits in being prepared for further international and Black and Minority Ethnic student recruitment by securing suitable provision at the institution for religion and belief needs of students.

Strengths
This approach is built around both anticipating need and responding to demand. A proactive approach ensures a more measured and strategic planned provision.

Weaknesses
Providing for anticipated need runs the risk of misdirecting expenditure of time and resource in areas where the need is not greatest. Studying the changes that have taken place in other HEIs both in the region, and in other Church HEIs across England and Wales reduces this risk.

Opportunities

This HEI Chaplaincy has the chance to develop some of the very first inter faith initiatives in the locality, and to be a positive influence in facilitating demographic change by ensuring an effective welcome to all. This could improve levels of student recruitment especially from areas in the wider region where the BME mix is showing signs of significant growth.

Threats

Sustaining such strategic developments requires the enthusiasm and vision of the existing chaplain and CEO. A lack of available energy or staff change could disrupt or halt development.

Next Steps: This development work is ongoing.

Findings
An HEI can improve its provision for the religious and belief needs of its members simply through making best use of the Christian chaplaincy, so long as the chaplaincy's intention is to serve the whole community, not just Christian faith adherents. The commitment by a Christian-led service to provide a facility for every HEI member is the norm rather than an exception. Having advisors or volunteers from different faith communities has many benefits and advantages. However a chaplaincy can still improve its provision without making a change from a Christian to an inter religious service.

Recommendations
Even a small chaplaincy staffed only by Christians can be effective in providing support and resource for the religious and belief needs in an HEI. Improving upon this in a measured and even-handed manner requires forethought and the commitment of working time for new developments. This can lead to influencing changes in recruitment of students and staff and change local demographics.

For further consideration
Where an institution recruits regionally, it is a simple task to assess what success the HEI is having in recruiting from a representative sample of the local population. Such analysis using 2001 census data can be instrumental in helping to foster some honesty about what target groups are being missed in the marketing and recruitment strategies of the HEI, and can lead to closer collaboration between the chaplaincy and those working in other areas of HEI public relations.

C15 Chaplaincy engagement with the local inter faith network

Type of activity	*Activity organiser(s)*
An HEI chaplaincy in a small city where fewer than 0.5% of the population are adherents to religions other than Christianity (according to the 2001 census) has sought to provide inter faith expertise and advice by participating in an existing inter faith centre and network.	The university chaplaincy and the local inter faith network, including the network's project director.

Involvement	*Context*
The faith communities of the city, the local inter faith project and its director and the university chaplaincy.	This post 1992 university in a small city has had a chaplaincy that has successfully provided representation from several Christian denominations for a considerable number of years. The chaplaincy service has served all students and staff, whatever their faith, tradition or beliefs. More recently, attention has been given to considering how such a chaplaincy can help to give further and more specific support to students of different religions and beliefs. Hence contact has been made with the local inter faith project.

Description: The director of the local inter faith project has been invited to participate in the chaplaincy by being a member of the staff team. This has resulted in a number of inter faith discussion evenings and lectures hosted in the chaplaincy. There have also been a number of visits to local faith communities' places of worship.

Strengths

In a city where there is only a small number of people from faith communities who are not Christians, the chaplaincy has succeeded in being in contact with, and supporting, local inter faith activity without taking on primary responsibility for the inter faith network. This has allowed the Chaplaincy to participate and support the existing project thus strengthening social cohesion.

Weaknesses

The chaplaincy is dependent on the success of an external organisation for its specific provision for world religions other than Christian.

Opportunities

The chaplaincy's approach in serving as a point of referral to local faith communities ensures that students and staff are given immediate access to those people who are most able to assist with specific religion and belief needs. The chaplaincy can retain its focus to serve the more generic needs of all students and staff in a way that is commensurate with the tradition of Christian ministry to people, whatever their religion or belief.

Threats

If the project ceased to operate this would have an impact on the chaplaincy provision. Similarly, either the departure of the current director or a change in the chaplaincy team that resulted in it being less sympathetic to collaboration could diminish or terminate the current collaboration.

Next Steps: The strength of the liaison has already created opportunities for inter religious events at the HEI. This may lead, in the future, to stronger liaison with the faith communities represented by the student and staff constituencies of the institution.

Findings
Contexts where local religious minorities are very small in number require a different type of approach so as effectively to:

- o   anticipate future need
- o   cater for the current small numbers of students and staff from the world religions
- o   encourage recruitment from a wider diversity of the population in the UK and internationally.

Recommendations

If an HEI is in a local setting with minimal ethnic diversity, it is most important to engage with the inter faith networks that do exist, however small they may be. If no such network already exists, the HEI should at least support, if not sponsor, the establishment of such an inter religious group. The chaplaincy described here did exactly that, and has benefited from being able to provide a more specialised service to a wider range of students and staff. It has also created the opportunity for fuller engagement in the local context. The importance of growing relationships with small faith communities cannot be emphasised too highly, if an HEI is committed to social cohesion and widening participation agendas.

For further consideration

Participating in existing collaboration or facilitating future liaison places the HEI in a strategic position, not only for developing its own provision, but also for helping to transform the local community. In places of greater religious and ethnic diversity there will be the opposite challenge of selecting the appropriate ways of networking and collaborating in a way that demonstrates equivalent and relevant interest in the variety of faith and inter faith groupings in the locality.

C16 Growing a fledgling 'multi-faith chaplaincy'

Type of activity	*Activity organiser(s)*
A new HEI has appointed a part-time chaplain in conjunction with the diocese to develop a 'multi-faith chaplaincy' as part of Student Services.	The new part-time chaplain in collaboration with colleagues.
Involvement	*Context*
The chaplain, the HEI in general and Student Services in particular, the Diocese, the advisory group and chaplaincy team members.	This urban redeveloping context is multi-racial and multi-ethnic. The profile of people who work and study at the HEI is highly diverse. The majority of students are mature and non-residential.

Description

The HEI, through dialogue with the local Anglican (Church of England) diocese, has very recently chosen to develop a chaplaincy service as part of Student Services. The intention is that this service will work to provide for the religious and belief needs of all students at least, and hopefully for staff as well.

Strengths

Starting virtually from scratch has enabled the lead chaplain to draw on exemplary practice from other institutions.

Weaknesses

A lack of funds, the slowness of HEI bureaucracy and part-time hours result in planned developments taking a considerable time to be realised.

Opportunities

It will be necessary to engage the local faith communities, the student societies and the student users of the prayer and quiet spaces at both campuses to deliver an effective service. The chaplain is unable to succeed alone due to the limited hours worked. However, because there is so little time available for the chaplain a collaborative approach to develop the service is guaranteed.

Threats

Such a small-scale operation may struggle to grow enough to be able to make effective provision for all faith communities in a coherent way. The chaplaincy role is part-time, whereas being the lead chaplain with responsibility for managing a team of volunteers easily fills the time of a full-time chaplain in the vast majority of other contexts.

Next steps
This process is ongoing.

Findings
HEIs are recognizing the valuable contribution of chaplaincy to institutional life because chaplaincy can:

- o   provide holistic services to support students' learning
- o   strengthen Student Services

Where HEIs are reconsidering the learning environment (see www.learningreconsidered.org), questions of inclusion and diversity become more significant.

External faith groups are glad to support new chaplaincies because

- o   they provide those of faith with support during their working day or time in study
- o   they create opportunities for sustained and stimulating relationships between religious and secular life.

Recommendations
Although it is understandable that taking the first step towards chaplaincy provision may not mean that employing a full-time member of staff is achievable, this can be counter-productive since it delays the fulfillment of aspirations for the service. It also limits the post-holder in developing inter religious co-operation as well as providing a service that is reactive, engaged and advisory. It also is highly likely that a part-time post-holder will be in a dual role. That can lead to difficulty in expanding the role, and can also prevent the post holder from guaranteeing a sustained focus when the other part of their work requires additional effort. Finding a source of further funding will provide a more than proportional benefit in terms of service development, flexibility and continuity.

For further consideration

Where choosing between a full or reduced-time appointment there may be merit in waiting up to a further year to secure enough sponsors for a full-time appointment, since the benefit is likely to be felt at the HEI within six months of the work beginning.

3. Conclusions and Next Steps

In this section a summary of the Project's findings (A), recommendations (B) and proposals for further consideration (C) is offered. Finally, some next steps (D) are suggested to help sustain and develop the inter religious collaboration that has both been uncovered by the current research and been generated by the project itself.

A. Findings

A1 Survey
The survey included the following findings.

- During the last five years 53% of chaplaincies have received new funding for existing and new activity.

- Chaplaincies that are thinking strategically are usually including provision for diverse religious needs in their priorities.

- There is a 95% consensus that it is necessary to make some provision for prayer spaces.

- Most new religious physical spaces at HEIs reflect the religious diversity of the student and staff population. 58% have multi-use prayer spaces, 51% have chapels and 65% have Muslim prayer rooms.

- 52% of chaplaincy staff are volunteers. Of those 371 volunteers, 31% (114) come from the Baha'i, Buddhist, Hindu, Jewish, Muslim, Sikh faiths.

- 75% of all voluntary and salaried chaplaincy staff are Christian. 95% of all salaried staff have a Christian role in their chaplaincy team.

- The majority of chaplaincies still use the word 'chaplaincy' as their name.

A2 Dialogues

Practitioner dialogues included the following findings.

- Inter religious teams are developing in many HEI chaplaincies.

- If faith and belief needs are to be understood better at an HEI, it is essential that there is closer collaboration by the chaplaincy with:
  - o local faith communities (including diverse strands and traditions)
  - o HE staff in other departments
  - o student faith societies.

- A responsive and proactive chaplaincy that is engaged with faith community concerns, as expressed locally and at the institution, makes a very valuable contribution to an HEI's identity. Having chaplaincy team members who can both represent their own faith effectively and who have a working knowledge of other faiths helps reduce the likelihood that needs will be overlooked (though how each HEI decides to engage with people from the full spectrum of religious and belief positions varies).

- Chaplaincies assist their HEIs with shaping vision and mission in relation to:
  - o building a holistic learning environment
  - o responding to internationalisation
  - o developing social cohesion
  - o promoting good relations
  - o improved access and participation
  - o collaborating for well being
  - o increasing community engagement.

- Volunteers are valuable and integrating appropriately skilled experts requires effective leadership and knowledge of existing best practice.

- Construction of new prayer spaces will not of itself ensure that an institution is making an equivalent provision for diverse religious and belief needs. However, prayer spaces may help by making relevant provision.

- A chaplain's (and faith community's) articulation of theology is always necessary, and inter religious team working requires further reflection.

- A few HEIs already provide modules in inter religious understanding. Some are optional and some are subject specific. Such teaching and learning promotes good relationships at HEIs.

A3 Narratives

The practice narratives included findings about the following.

- Built spaces for religious use have the potential both to validate and to marginalise, particularly in relation to:
  - different needs for space from diverse groups
  - difficulty in maintaining equal access to space (e.g. in relation to gender and timetabling, lunchtime pressure on a meeting space, a quieter group booked in a space in close proximity to a loud group).

- The main ways that chaplaincies and HEIs provide for diverse religious needs are through the provision of:
  - prayer space
  - volunteer chaplaincy staff.

- Students' own faith identities, and their assumptions about others, are likely to be challenged while at an HEI. Chaplaincies can play a significant role both in challenging expectations and supporting a person who finds his or her identity is challenged.

- Student faith societies make a substantial contribution to the expression of religious identity at an HEI. These societies are at their most successful when:
  - external groups are used for appropriate support
  - the Students' Union and chaplaincy liaise and collaborate with student-run societies.

- Responding to specific needs of different religious groups can be enhanced substantially by:
    - team working
    - the building of good relationships between faith communities
    - having experienced staff in place to facilitate the appropriate co-operation between those sharing facilities.

- HEIs situated in areas with a very limited diversity in the local population are faced with particular challenges when engaging with faith issues, because of a lack of opportunities for reciprocal support between faith communities and the institutions.

- Successful inter religious activities result from careful planning and consultation with the faith communities before during and after the activities take place.

B. Recommendations

B1 Survey

The following are among the recommendations that arose from the survey.

- HEIs should coordinate more inter religious activity in order to foster improved understanding between people from different religions.

- 'Multi-faith' is not a common term used to describe HEI chaplaincies and is avoided by some who nonetheless seek to develop good inter faith working in their chaplaincies. Such terminology should only be adopted after due consideration.

- Many HEIs now benefit from having more than one type of permanent prayer space. Those that have not created such spaces should consider the experience of those who have, and appropriately prioritise such provision in relation to other faith needs. An assessment of who benefits most from prayer space is important to ensure that all equalities strands (i.e. gender, sexuality, race, ethnicity, disability etc.) are being considered as provisions are put in place.

- Improving volunteer and part-time chaplaincy skills requires a change in national, regional and local training provision. Faith communities and sector providers should address this as a priority.

- Each HEI has the challenge of considering how they choose to respond to the religious and belief identities of students and staff who hold views other than those of the world religions. Those with responsibility for responding may include Equality and Diversity departments, Student Services or chaplaincies, and this will vary from institution to institution. Chaplaincies should be able to be effective in:

  - providing advice and guidance (resulting from awareness and research into the diverse religious and belief organisations in the locality; this should include seeking relevant information from national experts, such as INFORM)

- o   signposting to respected groups.

- Chaplaincies should note that there have been many successes in obtaining new money in recent years, and should consider making strategic funding applications to support their work.

B2 Dialogues

The following are among the recommendations that arose from the practice dialogues.

- Chaplaincies and HEIs should consider how effective specialist staff are at meeting the religion and belief needs of students and staff. HEIs aspiring to succeed in building good campus relationships will benefit from access to relevant expertise and should seek advice.

- It is essential that HEI senior management teams engage with chaplaincies when religion and belief topics are being considered. Three recommendations arise from this:

  - o   chaplains and chaplaincies should be willing and able carefully to articulate their purpose and expertise to the HEIs they serve

  - o   leaders, governors and managers in HEIs and faith communities should be champions for chaplaincy work.

- HEIs should include chaplaincies in consultation processes, alongside others, when institutional strategic aims are being set.

- Developing the skills of team leaders in coordinating teams and implementing best practice for volunteers is a priority. Those responsible for chaplains and chaplaincies should address this.

- The context in which a chaplaincy operates shapes the theology that develops. The complexity of HE creates a stimulating environment in which to develop a theology. Chaplaincy teams should be willing to make time to seek to understand the different theological perspectives held by colleagues.

- HEIs should recognise that chaplaincy work can support the process of personal development and help to foster a desire for mutual understanding between individuals and groups. An assessment should be made of whether there are further opportunities for chaplains to provide support and training of other HEI staff in responding to students' needs.

- Literacy about matters of religion and belief among the students and staff at an HEI assists in promoting good relationships between people holding diverse beliefs within an institution. New modules designed to be inter-disciplinary and address social, moral, cultural and spiritual issues would be beneficial for students and staff, and should be considered as part of curriculum design and staff development planning. Faculties, chaplaincies and staff development could all contribute to this.

- As HEIs develop their engagement with the local communities, local faith communities and employers, chaplaincies should be effective leaders in establishing relationships on behalf of HEIs with:
    - faith community leaders
    - faith community groups
    - religious experts
    - inter faith forums, activities and centres
    - other chaplaincies within the education sector at all
    - other chaplaincies across other sectors (including prisons, hospitals, armed services and workplaces).

    Such relationships should ensure a local recognition that the HEI of the diversity represented in the locality and enhance local communities, which in turn should assist students integrate into the wider community.

- HEIs should ensure that provisions for religious and belief needs do not disadvantage individuals on the basis of gender, disability, sexuality, race, ethnicity and social background.

B3 Narratives

The following are among the recommendations that arose from the practice narratives.

- HEIs should ensure that new facilities do not disadvantage individuals on the basis of gender, disability, sexuality, race and ethnicity.

- Building inter religious teams requires the fostering of sustained relationships with local faith communities. HEIs and faith communities should actively promote the development of such relationships.

- Chaplaincies that aspire to develop inter religious teams should consider recruiting volunteers as an effective next step.

- Liaison and consultation by chaplaincy staff with colleagues from other areas, student societies and with the local community lead to the potential for designing a more 'fit for purpose' service and chaplains should proactively seek such engagement.

- Inter religious co-operation and dialogue in each specific context should be encouraged in order to ensure that provisions at an HEI and in its chaplaincy are more closely matched to need (as opposed to taking on, unreflectively, models from other institutions). Where such dialogue takes place there is a higher likelihood that mutual listening and understanding can develop and enables the exchange of ideas in an academic environment. It also increases the chances that people with extreme views will come into contact with more moderate perspectives, which in turn serves the academic purposes of the exchange of ideas.

- Close attention should be paid to defining the most appropriate terms and conditions for voluntary employment.

- A 'one size fits all' approach to establishing new prayers facilities is unlikely to succeed. A common assumption is that space for prayer should be the first priority in responding to religion and belief needs. This is not necessarily the case.

- In order to promote better relations between diverse religious groups and individuals at an HEI through inter religious activities:

    o   chaplaincies should become an appropriate place for encounter between different groups
    o   student societies should be encouraged to liaise more closely with each other
    o   HEIs should run and support inter religious events themselves.

- HEIs and Students' Unions should support efforts by students to establish inter religious societies.

- Where the context is less diverse, HEIs should give the same attention to equitable provision for students with specific religion and belief needs as they should in a more obviously diverse context.

- When an HEI is involved in inter religious events a process of consultation and review should be established to assess the activity. This will ensure that those from different religions and beliefs are involved in defining what common activities are both appropriate and relevant for each occasion.

C. For further consideration

C1 Survey

The survey raises the following questions for further consideration.

- What are the advantages and disadvantages of changing the nomenclature of the title of a chaplaincy and the job titles of its staff?

- How valid are the reasons chaplaincies may be staffed only by Christians? These reasons may include:
  - confidence of the existing chaplaincy staff in offering support to all HEI members
  - the specific context
  - a lack of aspiration to change
  - a lack of contacts with other religions.

- What would be an equivalent level of staffing provision for different religions in any particular HEI? This is complex because aspirations are best set in relation to several factors:
  - numbers of faith adherents at the HEI
  - specific needs of respective groups
  - anticipation of future need
  - representation for religious and belief groups.

C2 Dialogues

The following matters for further consideration come from issues raised during the practice dialogues.

- How can an HEI chaplaincy engage more effectively with diverse groups in order to bring changes to local levels of inter religious co-operation, and improve community cohesion?

- If an HEI chooses to develop its vision in relation to religion and belief, can this be done so that there is a positive impact on its success with widening participation, employer engagement, community cohesion and promoting good relations at the institution?

- Might an HEI's market success depend in part on an effective response to religion and belief needs and aspirations of those who want to study and work in higher education?

- Will repositioning a chaplaincy service within an HEI's structures substantially alter perceptions of what a chaplaincy is for and how it can serve institutional aims, and will that be beneficial or detrimental?

- When new funding is sought, how can the meeting of *diverse* needs be anticipated in order to strengthen and enhance initial ideas for bids?

- It is possible to make some appropriate provisions without much inter religious collaboration. Where are the opportunities to go beyond provision to more substantial co-operation in order to guarantee the best outcomes from enhanced services and facilities?

- HEIs currently typically expect Christian chaplaincy staff to facilitate co-operation between diverse groups (which adds to the challenge of constructing a coherent Christian theology of chaplaincy). Where (in the majority of cases) those chaplains are funded by the churches, are there legitimate questions to be asked about the proportion of chaplains time spent coordinating wider teams, and should HEIs be more open to funding the coordination part of a chaplain's role even if they are unwilling to fund chaplaincy work itself?

- Are there ways of including 'social, cultural, moral and spiritual development' topics in the curriculum in a way that would help members of an academic community to develop a sophistication of discourse in addressing religion and belief issues?

- Can HEIs work with
    o   national chaplaincy advisors
    o   Universities UK
    o   GuildHE
    o   the Equality Challenge Unit
    o   the Association of Managers of Student Services in Higher Education (AMOSSHE)

- o National Union of Students
- o The Inter Faith Network for the UK

to draw up advice to ensure an individual's religion and belief needs are not ignored due to the specific strand or tradition they belong to within a religion or the specific beliefs the individual holds? Can HEIs work with the same groups to draw up advice to ensure individuals religion and belief needs are not ignored due to their gender, disability, sexuality, race, ethnicity, social background?

C3 Narratives

The practice narratives raise the following questions for further consideration.

- Many Christian chaplains are working in ecumenical groups. Transforming that setting into a team representing different religions requires a range of skills, patience and an investment of time. How can this best be resourced?

- Inter religious working together requires:
  - o clear team structures
  - o team building
  - o sophistication in dialogue.

  What commitments can an HEI and local faith communities undertake to support this painstaking development work?

- Inter religious events are powerful expressions of how space can be made and shared between people who hold diverse perspectives and yet hold common values. How can HEIs, chaplaincies and faith communities best work together to enable a process of education to develop the religious literacy of students and staff that will in turn create an environment where more members of an HEI will be both amenable to and supportive of such occasions?

D. Next Steps

Arising out of all that has gone before, due consideration should be given to the following:

D1 A national Inter Religious Working Group

Arising from the consultation that has taken place during the work of this project with representatives from nine world faiths, the HE sector, the practitioner groups and interested parties (including the Inter Faith Network, the National Union of Students, Universities UK, GuildHE and the Equality Challenge Unit), it would be possible and practical to set up a national working group to continue to give further consideration to the issues that have been raised in this report. A quarterly meeting would help maintain a momentum in considering how faith communities can engage with the HE sector, especially through chaplaincies. The Working Group would require adequate funding to be viable.

D2 A national Faiths in Higher Education Forum

The findings of a national working group could provide the suitable context and relevant content to equip a national 'Faiths in HE Forum'. The working group would make invitations to the principal representatives from the world religions, with a brief for HE, to join the forum. This would effectively bring experts together to consider the opportunities for holistic learning and positive relationships between diverse religious groups participating in higher education. It would also establish a context where common concerns held by faith communities, the HE sector and related government departments could be shared.

D3 Funding for a Faiths in Higher Education Development Officer

A funded development officer would be able to service, advise and sustain the activity of the national Working Group and Forum.

D4 Training

This report has clearly identified training needs for chaplaincy staff and also indicates the value of further equipping of HEI leaders and managers who are considering issues of religion and belief at their institution.

Training is partly the responsibility of the faith communities who provide chaplains, and partly that of HEIs. But the existence of the above mentioned Forum and Working Group could also better enable the production of training materials to include:

- o fact-sheets on some of the basic religion and belief needs of student and staff
- o web-based training in a tool-kit style
- o training events for chaplaincy staff, leaders, governors and managers
- o if resources allow, bespoke training for individual HEIs.

D5 Guidance

Guidance that is considered and written collaboratively is urgently needed as follows:

- o Further advice on how to develop dialogue as a way of resisting religious intolerance and challenging extreme perspectives
- o Further advice on how equitability (or dynamic equivalence) can be built into provision for the faiths
- o Advice on possibilities for increasing the number of salaried religious professionals working in chaplaincies from all the faith communities
- o Ensuring consideration of the suitability of existing faiths provision for people in an HEI who belong to a specific strand or tradition within a world religion that may be marginalised
- o Ensuring access to religion and belief provision for those who may currently be disadvantaged due to their gender, disability, sexuality, race, ethnicity, social background etc.
- o Increasing the opportunities for inter religious dialogue
- o Increasing the opportunities for dialogue between people who hold diverse religious and belief perspectives
- o Suggestions on how it could be appropriate to collect voluntarily provided data from students about their religion or belief alongside the ethnicity data they already provide.

Best advice will be that which is drawn up, in dialogue, by experts in the field such as national chaplaincy advisors, Universities UK, GuildHE, the Equality Challenge Unit, the Association of Managers of Student Services in Higher Education (AMOSSHE), the National Union of Students and the Inter Faith Network, drawing on the experience of their various members and networks.

Afterword

As Principal of King's College London I want to welcome this Report. King's College London was founded by King George IV and the Duke of Wellington (then Prime Minister) in 1829 as a university college in the tradition of the Church of England. It now welcomes staff and students of all faiths and beliefs, and is one of the oldest and largest colleges of the University of London with 13,000 undergraduate students and some 6,200 postgraduate students, in nine schools of study. While continuing the Christian tradition with daily worship in the College's Chapels, the Dean and Chaplaincy also seek to serve the religious needs of all staff and students, with the result that we now have dedicated Muslim Prayer Rooms on each of our sites, the Rabbi to Jewish Students visits as an accredited member of the Chaplaincy team, and there are a number of student religious societies encompassing the major faith communities, including the Buddhist Society, the Christian Union, the Hindu Society, the Islamic Society, the Jewish Society, and the Sikh Society. All this has enabled us at King's to deal with issues of religious identity and pluralism in a context of open discussion and sharing, particularly post-7/7.

As a result of our experiences, I welcome the evidence in this Report which suggests that working together to consider the needs and rich contributions of all the faith communities to the Higher Education sector will be beneficial to all students and staff, and that Chaplaincies have a key role to play in Higher Education Institutions in this respect. I am also glad to see the suggestion that there should be further consultation soon by interested parties to reflect on the findings and recommendations together and to prioritise further action.

Professor Rick Trainor
Principal, King's College London

Appendix 1: Literature Review

This section gives a brief review of how the findings of this project relate to relevant earlier publications that address issues in higher education chaplaincy.

1. Sophie Gilliat-Ray (1999), *Higher Education and Student Religious Identity.*

Sophie Gilliat-Ray's report has similarities in its findings on the following topics:

- o Most religious professionals working in chaplaincies are Christian (p. 15).
- o Buddhist, Jewish and Muslim involvement in chaplaincy was noted (p. 15).
- o Provisions for prayer are being made for people from different faith communities (p. 17).

Differences between her findings and those of this project are:

- o No Baha'i, Hindu or Sikh involvement in chaplaincy was discovered (p. 15). The present project, however, has discovered Baha'i, Hindu and Sikh involvement.
- o A quarter of chaplaincies surveyed noted some inter faith activity taking place at their HEI (p. 27). The present project notes, however, that nearly three quarters of chaplaincies noted some inter faith activity at their HEI(s).

2. Giles LeGood, ed. (1999), *Chaplaincy: The Church's Sector Ministries.*

In this edited volume there is a chapter by Giles himself ('Universities', pp. 132-140). In this, he examines the history of higher education chaplaincy in the UK, discusses some theological themes that may underpin it and explores how what is believed about God and the world shapes the way chaplaincy operates. This is written about Christian chaplaincy from a Christian theological standpoint, and while it is a helpful exploration in itself, it makes no reference to chaplains of other faiths, or to university chaplaincy work beyond Christian ministry. His efforts at articulating a theology of Christian chaplaincy are complemented by the practice dialogue 'The Christian chaplain as theologian in an HE inter faith context' where the complexity of the setting in which a chaplain has to operate is expanded upon.

3. General Synod of the Board of Education (2002) *Pillars of the Church: supporting chaplaincy in further and higher education.*

Pillars of the Church devotes just one paragraph to inter religious issues (p. 25), noting that 'chaplaincies vary enormously in their response to this matter, sometimes depending on the attitude of the college involved or the outlook of the individual chaplain'.

The current project, on the other hand, invited practitioners to share their views, and the findings indicate significant common ground and some diversity. The comprehensive survey conducted suggests many ways in which there is a consistent response to inter religious working and responding to the needs of diverse faith groups.

4. Simon Robinson (2004), *Ministry Among Students: A Pastoral Theology and Handbook for Practice.*

Simon Robinson has a brief section on inter faith issues (pp. 86-88) where he speaks of a pressure from HEIs for chaplaincies to 'network effectively with other faiths' (p. 86) and argues that 'it is not possible to have a chaplaincy in which other faiths play an inclusive or organisational role'. He does, however, suggest inter religious liaison and support for faith awareness activities and regular meetings between faith leaders to monitor 'faith and pastoral relationships'. His analysis is not substantiated with any specific research, and although it reflects some concerns of practitioners during this project, our findings suggest that working together in collaborative teams is both possible and beneficial.

5. Church of England Board of Education (2005), *Aiming Higher: Higher Education and the Church's Mission.*

In *Aiming Higher* it is established early on that 'the very diversity of higher education provides a safe context in which difference can be explored, intolerance countered and beliefs questioned' (3.6). This point is expanded further in the statement that 'this creates opportunities for people of faith to explore their beliefs in a wider context and to interact with each other' (5.2). The report then introduces the relevance of employment legislation (8.1) explaining that 'this is affecting how some institutions are thinking about ways they engage with the faiths'. It continues by outlining the 'spiritual and practical' needs of international students (8.2) and suggests that HEIs will value chaplaincies that provide a service that is 'explicitly for all' (8.3). Where chaplaincies have (8.3),

> taken initiative in helping the university to ensure that the community's diverse faith needs are met, this has been invaluable in establishing [the chaplaincy's] credibility in the institution. At the same time, ensuring that students and staff can be supported in other faith traditions can release Christian chaplains to be explicitly Christian alongside others expressing their own faiths.

The dialogues on 'Faith communities as HEI stakeholders' and 'HEI mission and vision' and the conclusions section of this report all expand on the points in *Aiming Higher* and then substantiate them.

6. Peter McGrail and John Sullivan (2005), *Dancing on the Edge: A Report into Catholic Chaplaincy in Higher Education.*

Dancing on the Edge suggests that the most significant element of inter faith chaplaincy in recent years is Islam (p. 48). The report provides, in contrast to Simon Robinson, research from a number of HEI chaplaincies and notes a diverse set of approaches to inter faith working (p. 49). McGrail and Sullivan indicate that 'establishing genuine multi-faith chaplaincies will not be an easy task' due to diverse perspectives on the role of chaplain and the requirement for a deepened understanding of one another arising out of dialogue (p. 49). Moving towards an inter faith model of chaplaincy, it is argued will require, additionally, significant reflection and dialogue (p. 50) and a change in approach from Catholic chaplains that will require them to give more time to collaboration rather than to concentrating on catholic students (p. 51).

The findings of McGrail and Sullivan reflect some of the views shared by practitioners in the present report (see especially the practice dialogues on volunteers, inter faith ethics for chaplaincy and student faith societies). *Faiths in Higher Education Chaplaincy* has found that some chaplaincies have made more substantial progress than *Dancing on the Edge* suggests the Church is equipped for or involved with.

7. Ataullah Siddiqui (2007), *Islam at Universities in England: Meeting the Needs and Investing in the Future.*

In *Islam at Universities*, Ataullah Siddiqui explores what the chaplaincy needs of Muslim students are ('Chaplaincy and Muslims', pp. 44-54). He suggests that the role of a chaplain or advisor is to be able to 'minister in the broadest sense to anyone, of any faith or none, who seeks guidance or support' and he goes on to speak of the role requiring not just knowledge of doctrine but also 'the ability to listen and support with moral attentiveness and yet do so non-judgementally' (p. 44). Siddiqui suggests there are 'perhaps over 30' (p. 46) Muslim chaplains working in HEIs in England (which is very close to the figure given in this report of 33 for England and Wales).

The funding of Muslim 'chaplain/advisor' posts, the process of making appointments, and of training prior to appointment are all discussed by Siddiqui (pp. 46-48). This relates to the concern raised in this report in Conclusion and Next Steps (D5) about how new funding can be obtained for salaried chaplains from the world faiths that are less well represented in HE chaplaincies. He then goes on to summarise four areas of student need that chaplaincy can serve:

- o 'Spiritual needs' (p. 48)
- o 'Counselling and emotional needs' (pp. 48-49)
- o 'Educational (religious specific) needs' (pp. 49-50)
- o 'Need for continuity and point of contact' (p. 50).

These same needs are reiterated many times in the findings of practitioners as summarised in the results of *Faiths in Higher Education Chaplaincy*.

In a section entitled 'difficulties of inter-faith chaplaincy' (pp. 50-52) Siddiqui highlights the significance of the theology of the lead Christian chaplain in an inter religious team. He points out that a theologically liberal chaplain may be less accepted by members of his or her own tradition (p. 51) and that a more leader more inclined to 'fundamentalist/exclusivist methods [...] may see the service as exclusively Christian, which can lead to the exclusion of the Muslim chaplain from the wider workings of the chaplaincy'. This finding relates to some of the perspectives offered in this present report by practitioners engaging in the topics of 'The Christian chaplain as theologian in an HE inter faith context' and 'An inter faith ethic for HE chaplaincy'. Siddiqui then outlines the argument for Muslim chaplaincies that operate independently of the Christian chaplaincy (pp. 50-52). This runs counter to the perspectives offered by practitioners in the present report.

Siddiqui concludes, however, with a contrasting quotation from a Muslim chaplain/advisor involved in inter faith chaplaincy, who argues for coherence in chaplaincy provision.

> A cohesive inter-faith chaplaincy in further/higher education should proactively establish sound relationships with all university religious and cultural societies. In order to establish such extensive networks the

chaplain(s) must ensure [that] a safe and welcoming environment exists within the chaplaincy, being aware and sensitive to the needs of people of different faiths and cultures is key to the success of an inter-faith chaplaincy (p. 54).

Similarly to the present report, Siddiqui seeks to offer the contrasting perspectives and approaches to chaplaincy rather than claiming that a single approach will always be best practice. He does, though, offer some very clear minimum standards for those preparing to work as Muslim chaplains/advisors as follows:

1. A good knowledge of Islam, preferably some kind of formal Islamic qualification.
2. Understanding of British society and university culture.
3. Understanding of other faiths and willingness to engage with them positively.
4. Communication and counselling skills and willingness to listen and be approachable.
5. Being open to all denominations within Islam (p. 53).

The third point from this list gives a clear message that inter religious working will be an important aspect of a Muslim chaplain/advisor's role. This point is made carefully and conclusively. This emphasis on seeking to deepen understanding of different faiths and to engage positively concurs with the findings and recommendations in *Faiths in Higher Education Chaplaincy*.

Appendix 2: Project participants

Faith Community representatives

Fatma Amer	Markfield Institute of Higher Education, Leicester
Aviva Dautch	Board of Deputies
Adam Dawson	National Jewish Chaplaincy Board
Gerry Devlin	Catholic Education Services
Kanwaljit Kaur Singh	Network of Sikh Organisations
Jay Lakhani	Hindu Council UK (consulted March 2007)
Sam McBratney	The Methodist Church
Melinda Michelson-Carr	Liberal Judaism
Mudita	Network of Buddhist Organisations
Mohammed Rafi	Muslim Council of Britain
Chris Ward	Network of Buddhist Organisations
Judith Williams	Reform Judaism

Telephone Survey respondents

Les Acklam	University of Lincoln
Rod Anderson	University of Bradford
Ian Arch	University of Chester
Gavin Ashenden	University of Sussex
Dean Ayres	Thames Valley University
Stuart Bell	Prifysgol Aberystwyth/University of Aberystwyth
Angela Berners-Wilson	University of Bath
Terry Biddington	University of Manchester, The Manchester Metropolitan University and the Royal Northern College of Music
Mark Bratton	University of Warwick
Stan Brown	Kingston University
Bernard Burke	The Manchester Metropolitan University
Richard Burridge	Kings College London
John Butler	Prifysgol Bangor/Bangor University
Benedict Cambridge	Staffordshire University
Malcolm Chamberlain	University of Liverpool
David Cherry	University of Westminster

Nils Chittenden	University of Durham
Peter Clarke	Trinity and All Saints College, Leeds
Paul Collier	Goldsmiths College, London
Nigel Cooper	Anglia Ruskin University
Christopher Cullwick	York St John University
Elaine Dando	University College London
Richard Davey	Nottingham Trent University
Tony Dickinson	Buckinghamshire Chilterns University College
Owen Dobson	Marjon (University College Plymouth St Mark and St John)
Roy Dorey	Heythrop College, London
Phil Edwards	University of Bolton
David Evans	University of Plymouth
Stephen Fagbemi	University of Sunderland
Paul Filmer	University of Greenwich
Jonathan Frost	University of Surrey
Jules Gomes	University of Greenwich; Trinity College of Music (Greenwich)
Ian Gommersall	University of Manchester
David Goodall	University of Bristol
Clifton Graham	University of Central England (now Birmingham City University)
Heather Greenwood	University of Northampton
Ainsley Griffiths	Coleg y Drindod Caerfyrddin/Trinity College Carmarthen
William Gulliford	Courtauld Institute of Art, London
Charles Hadley	University of Exeter
Richard Hall	Prifysgol Abertawe/University of Swansea
Stephen Heap	University of Bedfordshire
Samuel Helkvist	Prifysgol Cymru Llanbedr Pont Steffan/University of Wales, Lampeter
Chris Hodder	University of Derby
Margaret Holland	Newman College of Higher Education, Birmingham
Andrew Howard	University of Teesside
Cassandra Howes	University of the West of England, Bristol
Kevin Huggett	University of Lancaster
Hadge Hughes	University of Chichester
Frank Hung	London South Bank University
Paul Hutchinson	University of Central Lancashire

Carolyn James	Bishop Grosseteste University College Lincoln
Nigel John	Prifysgol Abertawe/University of Swansea
Janice Jones	Athrofa Addysg Uwch Gogledd Ddwyrain Cymru/North East Wales Institute of Higher Education
Peter Jones	University of Portsmouth
Robert Jones	Roehampton University, London
Amos Kasibante	University of Leicester
Caroline Kennedy	University of Central Lancashire
Janet Knott	Bath Spa University
Catherine Lack	University of Keele
Stephen Laird	University of Kent
Will Lamb	University of Sheffield
Jeremy Law	Canterbury Christ Church University
Colin Lawlor	University of Brighton
Jonathan Lawson	University of Durham—College of St Hild and St Bede
Mark Laynesmith	University of Reading
Giles Legood	Royal Veterinary College/Royal Free and University College
Nicholas lo Polito	University of Birmingham
David Mackenzie Mills	University of Cambridge
Ian Maher	Sheffield Hallam University
Andy Marshall	Southampton Solent University
Sam McBratney	City University
Jennifer McCoach	Coventry University
Darren McFarland	University of Paisley
Tamsin Merchant	University of Gloucestershire
Ivor Moody	Anglia Ruskin University
Anthony Moore	Royal Academy of Music
Stephen Nicholson	University of York
Andrew Norwood	University of the Arts London
Jonnie Parkin	De Montfort University
Mike Peatman	St Martin's College, Lancaster (now University of Cumbria)
David Peebles	London School of Economics and Political Science
Emma Pennington	Worcester College, Oxford
Jenny Petersen	Queen Mary, University of London
Matthew Pollard	University of Huddersfield

Vaughan Rees	Prifysgol Morgannwg/University of Glamorgan
Simon Richardson	Loughborough University
Charles Sargent	Brunel University
Steven Shakespeare	Liverpool Hope University
Allan Smith	University of Hertfordshire
Judith Stephenson	University of Hull
Simon Stevens	University of Southampton
Simon Talbott	University College for the Creative Arts
Ian Tarrant	University of Nottingham
Moray Thomas	Goodenough College, London
Darren Thornton	University of East Anglia
Howard Thornton	University of Bedfordshire
Mark Vasey Saunders	University of Newcastle upon Tyne
Alex Walt	University of Essex
Matt Ward	University of Leeds and Leeds Metropolitan University
Kim Wasey	University of Salford
Jonathan Watkins	University of Winchester
Fiona Weaver	London Metropolitan University
Rose Westwood	University College Falmouth and University of Exeter (Cornwall Campus)
Margaret Whipp	Oxford Brookes University
Andrew Wilson	Imperial College London
Gavin Wort	University of Northumbria at Newcastle
Sally Wright	Guildhall School of Music and Drama
Geoffrey Wynne	University of Wolverhampton

Practice Dialogue participants

Les Acklam	University of Lincoln
Sheila Ainsley Smith	The Manchester Metropolitan University
Jan Ainsworth	Diocese of Manchester
Karin Alderson	University of Newcastle upon Tyne
Fatma Amer	The Markfield Institute of Higher Education, Leicester
Rod Anderson	University of Bradford and Bradford College
Ruth Appleton	Bournemouth University
David Arblaster	Leeds Metropolitan University
Ian Arch	University of Chester

Nick Baker	University of Leeds and Leeds Metropolitan University
Leslie M Barrett	University of Abertay, Dundee
Terry Biddington	Manchester University, The Manchester Metropolitan University and the Royal Northern College of Music
Stan Brown	Kingston University
Maureen Burke	University of Glasgow, University of Strathclyde and Glasgow Caledonian University
Benedict Cambridge	Staffordshire University
Jeremy Clines	Education Division, Church of England
Lucille Cohen	University of Manchester
Paul Collier	Goldsmiths College
Nigel Cooper	Anglia Ruskin University
Richard Davey	Nottingham Trent University
David V Evans	University of Plymouth
Stephen Fagbemi	University of Sunderland
Paul Filmer	University of Greenwich and University College for the Creative Arts
David F Ford	University of Cambridge
Jonathan Frost	University of Surrey
Alex Goldberg	University of Surrey
David Goodall	University of Bristol
Heather Greenwood	University of Northampton
Henry Guterman	Manchester Jewish community
Nasreen Hanif	University of Manchester
Ron Hart	University of the West of England, Bristol
Margaret Holland	Newman College of Higher Education, Birmingham
Cassandra Howes	University of the West of England, Bristol
Hadge Hughes	University of Chichester
Geoff Hunt	University of Surrey
David Hutchison	University of Aberdeen
Paul Jeorrett	Athrofa Addysg Uwch Gogledd Ddwyrain Cymru/North East Wales Institute of Higher Education
Zishan Jiwa	University of Cambridge
Janice Jones	Athrofa Addysg Uwch Gogledd Ddwyrain Cymru/North East Wales Institute of Higher Education
Peter Jones	University of Portsmouth

Robert Kaggwa	Digby Stuart College, Roehampton University, London
Ann Keating	University of Winchester
Mary Kenefick	London Metropolitan University
Jenna Khulsan	NUS (National Union of Students)
Karolina Kopiec	University of Manchester Students' Union
Will Lamb	University of Sheffield
Carol Lanham	Goldsmiths College, London
Jonathan Lawson	College of St Hild and St Bede, University of Durham
Tara Leach	University of Salford
Michael Lewis	Diocese of Manchester
Sharon Lusty	York St John University
Stuart D MacQuarrie	University of Glasgow
Bill Matthews	University of Portsmouth
Philip Maybank	University of Durham
John McCarthy	University of Surrey
Ruth McLeod	University of Surrey
Khan Moghal	Manchester Council for Community Relations
Duncan Myers	Hatfield College, Durham University
Sogra Newman	Anglia Ruskin University
Lukas Njenga	Glasgow Caledonian University
Andrew Norwood	University of the Arts London
Gareth Powell	Prifysgol Caerdydd/Cardiff University
James Ramsay	University of East London
Vaughan Rees	Prifysgol Morgannwg/University of Glamorgan
Steven Shakespeare	Liverpool Hope University
Hugh Shilson-Thomas	Education Division, Church of England
Allan Smith	University of Hertfordshire
Pat Sponder	University of Manchester
Sarah Talcott	University of Surrey
Geoffrey Walker	Whitelands College, Roehampton University
Julie Walkling	London Metropolitan University
Kim Wasey	University of Salford
Fiona Weaver	London Metropolitan University
Rose Westwood	University College Falmouth and University of Exeter (Cornwall Campus)
Margaret Whipp	Oxford Brookes University
Andrew Willson	Imperial College, London
Mo Yu-In	Manchester Baha'i community

Critical Readers

Jan Ainsworth
Fatma Amer
Harriet Crabtree
Moussa Haddad
Alice Hynes
Barney Leith
Catherine Marston
Melinda Michelson-Carr
Alan Murray
Susan O'Brien
Natubhai Shah
Anna Thomas-Betts
Chris Ward
Guy Wilkinson

Those who have given guidance, additional information and support to the project

Rod Anderson
Gwyn Arnold
Terry Biddington
Mark Bratton
Stan Brown
Richard Burridge
Benedict Cambridge
David Chiddick
David Clines
Harriet Crabtree
Les Ebdon
David Evans
Alexander Fostiropoulos
Jonathan Frost
David Goodall
Charles Hadley
Christian Heycocks
Cassandra Howes
Hadge Hughes
Stuart Jennings

Gareth Jones
Rob Jones
Kanwaljit Kaur-Singh
Will Lamb
Jonathan Lawson
Michael Lewis
Sharon Lusty
Ian Maher
Ian Millgate
Rachel Moriarty
Andrew Norwood
Nicholas lo Polito
Brian Pearce
James Ramsay
Rees Rawlings
Vaughan Rees
Muir Russell
Ataullah Siddiqui
Indarjit Singh
Sarah Talcott
Fran Tate
Anthony Thiselton
Anna Thomas-Betts
Rick Trainor
Stephen Venner
Jonathan Watkins
Fiona Weaver
Guy Wilkinson
Dianne Willcocks
Michael Worton

Appendix 3: Visits to chaplaincies and HEIs

The Project Officer visited:

University of the Arts, London
University of Birmingham
University of Bradford
University of Bristol
University of Cambridge
University of Chichester
Coleg y Drindod Caerfyrddin/Trinity College, Carmarthen
University of Durham
University of East London
University of Exeter
Kingston University
London Metropolitan University
University of Manchester
Manchester Metropolitan University
Marjon (University College Plymouth St Mark and St John)
Markfield Institute of Higher Education, Leicester
Coleg Mihangel Sant/St Michael's College, Llandaff
University of Plymouth
University of Sheffield
Sheffield Hallam University
Staffordshire University
University of Surrey
University of Warwick
University of the West of England, Bristol
University of Winchester
York St John University

Appendix 4: Telephone survey questionnaire

1. Name of interviewee?
2. E-mail?
3. Direct telephone line?
4. Job title of interviewee?
5. Name of institution?
6. What is the Chaplaincy service called?
7. How many paid full-time staff?
8. What are the job titles of the paid full-time staff?
9. How many paid part-time staff?
10. What are the job titles of the paid part-time staff?
11. How many voluntary staff work in a religious capacity for the university/college?
12. What are the job titles of the voluntary staff?
13. In addition to the staff are there other contacts, links or external advisors that are advertised as part of your service; if so, how many?
14. What are the role titles for your contacts, links and external advisors?
15. How many sacred spaces are there, dedicated or consecrated as Chapels?
16. How many permanent prayer spaces are there for the exclusive use of Muslims?
17. How many other permanent spaces are there for quiet and prayer for use by all or some?
18. Are there any temporary spaces used for prayer or worship? Please describe?
19. What other space is there for the religious staff and volunteers of the university/college?
20. How many different religions are represented by student societies?
21. Are there any non-curricular inter religious societies at the university/college?
22. Are there any non-curricular inter religious events that happen at the university/college?
23. What is the nature of the inter religious societies? Please can you give a brief description?

24. What is the nature of the inter religious events? Please can you give a brief description?
25. Are there any development plans, targets, protocol or strategic aims for provision for students and staff of faith at the university/college?
26. Has any new funding been sought for provision for students and staff of faith in the last five years?
27. Has any funding been received to develop provision for students and staff of faith?

Appendix 5: Building Good Relations with People of Different Faiths and Beliefs

Explanatory note: This appendix reproduces the text of a publication by the Inter Faith Network for the UK (IFN). The full version also contains a list of 111 member organisations of the IFN. These member organisations are listed under four categories: Faith Community Representative Bodies, Interfaith Organisations, Local Inter Faith Bodies and Educational and Academic Bodies.

The Inter Faith Network for the UK was established in 1987 to promote good relations between the faith communities of this country. This code is endorsed by all its member bodies.

Building Good Relations with People of Different Faiths and Beliefs

In Britain today, people of many different faiths and beliefs live side by side. The opportunity lies before us to work together to build a society rooted in the values we treasure. But this society can only be built on a sure foundation of mutual respect, openness and trust. This means finding ways to live our lives of faith with integrity, and allowing others to do so too. Our different religious traditions offer us many resources for this and teach us the importance of good relationships characterised by honesty, compassion and generosity of spirit. The Inter Faith Network offers the following code of conduct for encouraging and strengthening these relationships.

As members of the human family, we should show each other respect and courtesy. In our dealings with people of other faiths and beliefs this means exercising good will and:

- Respecting other people's freedom within the law to express their beliefs and convictions

- Learning to understand what others actually believe and value, and letting them express this in their own terms

- Respecting the convictions of others about food, dress and social etiquette and not behaving in ways which cause needless offence

- Recognising that all of us at times fall short of the ideals of our own traditions and never comparing our own *ideals* with other people's *practices*

- Working to prevent disagreement from leading to conflict

- Always seeking to avoid violence in our relationships

When we talk about matters of faith with one another, we need to do so with sensitivity, honesty and straightforwardness. This means:

- Recognising that listening as well as speaking is necessary for a genuine conversation

- Being honest about our beliefs and religious allegiances

- Not misrepresenting or disparaging other people's beliefs and practices

- Correcting misunderstanding or misrepresentations not only of our own but also of other faiths whenever we come across them

- Being straightforward about our intentions

- Accepting that in formal inter faith meetings there is a particular responsibility to ensure that the religious commitment of all those who are present will be respected.

All of us want others to understand and respect our views. Some people will also want to persuade others to join their faith. In a multi faith society where this is permitted, the attempt should always be characterised by self-restraint and a concern for the other's freedom and dignity. This means:

- Respecting another person's expressed wish to be left alone

- Avoiding imposing ourselves and our views on individuals or communities who are in vulnerable situations in ways which exploit these

- Being sensitive and courteous.

- Avoiding violent action or language, threats, manipulation, improper inducements, or the misuse of any kind of power

- Respecting the right of others to disagree with us

Living and working together is not always easy. Religion harnesses deep emotions which can sometimes take destructive forms. Where this happens, we must draw on our faith to bring about reconciliation and understanding. The truest fruits of religion are healing and positive. We have a great deal to learn from one another which can enrich us without undermining our own identities. Together, listening and responding with openness and respect, we can move forward to work in ways that acknowledge genuine differences but build on shared hopes and values.

Building Good Relations with People of Different Faiths and Beliefs © The Inter Faith Network for the UK 1993, 2005

www.interfaith.org.uk

Bibliography

Church of England Board of Education
    2002   *Pillars of the Church: supporting chaplaincy in further and higher education*, Church House Publishing, London.
    2005   *Aiming Higher: Higher Education and the Church's Mission*, Church House Publishing, London.
    2005   *Mutual Expectations: The Church of England and Church Colleges/ Universities*, Church House Publishing, London.

Equality Challenge Unit
    2007   *Promoting Good Campus Relations: An Institutional Imperative*, Update Guidance, Equality Challenge Unit, London.

Gilliat-Ray, Sophie
    1999   *Higher Education and Student Religious Identity*, Department of Sociology, University of Exeter in association with the Inter Faith Network for the UK, Exeter.

Graham, Gordon
    2005   *The Institution of Intellectual Values: Realism and Idealism in Higher Education*, Imprint Academic, Exeter.

Inter-Faith Consultative Group (Mission and Public Affairs Council)
    2005   *Presence and Engagement: the church's task in a multi Faith society*, Church House Publishing, London.

The Inter Faith Network for the UK
    2005   *Building Good Relations with People of Different Faiths and Beliefs* (2nd edition), The Inter Faith Network for the UK, London.

The Inter Faith Network for the UK (in association with the Equality Challenge Unit)
    2007   *Building Good Relations on Campus*, The Inter Faith Network for the UK, London.

Jenkins, Timothy
    2006   *An Experiment in Providence: How Faith Engages the World*, SPCK Publishing, London.

LeGood, Giles
    1999   'Universities' in *Chaplaincy: The Church's Sector Ministries* by Giles LeGood, Cassell, London.

LeGood, Giles (ed.)
1999   *Chaplaincy: The Church's Sector Ministries*, Cassell, London.

McGrail, Peter and John Sullivan
2005   *Dancing on the Edge: A Report into Catholic Chaplaincy in Higher Educa-tion*, a report produced for the Conference of Catholic Chaplain in Higher Education.
2007   *Dancing on the Edge: Chaplaincy, Church and Higher Education*, Matthew James Publishing, Chelmsford.

National Ecumenical Agency in Further Education (NEAFE) and the Faiths in Further Education Forum
2007   *Making Space for Faith: Values, Beliefs and Faiths in the Learning and Skills Sector*, NEAFE and Centre for Excellence in Leadership (CEL), London.

Pattison, Stephen
2007   *Challenge of Practical Theology*, Jessica Kingsley Publishers, London.

Robinson, Simon
2004   *Ministry Among Students: A Pastoral Theology and Handbook for Prac-tice*, Canterbury Press Norwich, Norwich.

Siddiqui, Ataullah
2007   *Islam at Universities in England: Meeting the Needs and Investing in the Future*, a Report submitted to Bill Rammell MP (Minster of State for Lifelong Learning, Further and Higher Education).

Sykes, Stephen
2006   *Power and Christian Theology*, Continuum, London.

Thatcher, Adrian (ed.)
1999   *Spirituality and the Curriculum*, Cassell, London.

Universities UK, GuildHE and the Equality Challenge Unit
2005   *Promoting Good Campus Relations: Dealing with Hate Crimes and Intol-erance*, Equality Challenge Unit, London.

Printed in the United Kingdom
by Lightning Source UK Ltd.
129754UK00001B/88-279/A

9 780955 809606